Walking in the Same Direction

Jeanne Hinton

Walking in the Same Direction

A New Way of Being Church

WCC Publications, Geneva

Cover design: Edwin Hassink

ISBN 2-8254-1160-4

© 1995 WCC Publications, World Council of Churches,
150 route de Ferney, 1211 Geneva 2, Switzerland

No. 67 in the Risk Book Series

Printed in Switzerland

To Richard and Sue,
Bob and Rachel,
another generation,
who are also walking
in the same direction

Contents

Foreword

Writing this book has been a journey for me. Again and again I have been moved and challenged by the stories that are told here, stories already familiar to me. Part of my work is gathering stories, especially of basic Christian communities that are discovering "a new way of being church". In that process you come to feel a part of many different communities; their stories become yours too. As indeed I feel them to be — my story and yours and that of many others who are also taking steps in this same direction.

The communities whose stories are told in the book are known by many different names and abbreviations; indeed, a bewildering variety — Basic Ecclesial Community (BEC), Basic Christian Community (BCC), Small Christian Community (SCC), Small Faith Community (SFC), Christian Popular Community (CPC), to name a few. The choice of such names is not an arbitrary one; each name has its own significance, as will become apparent in reading the stories. But there is also a common thread throughout: a new way of being church that is emerging from "the base" — from the poor and marginalized, from the grassroots. It is emerging among ordinary lay Christians who are working out their faith in everyday life, discovering what an authentic Christian life-style should mean in today's world, what it means to be church, to rediscover Christian community. Many church leaders and theologians see in these basic Christian communities the church of the future. Arising first here, then there, not globally in any planned way but with a spontaneity that characterizes all work of the Spirit, and with an influence on both society and church that is out of all proportion to their strength and numbers. In such a way change happens. Not all at once, but gradually, little by little.

When I started work on this book I looked in alarm at the mass of paper, magazines, reports and books on the shelves and the floor of my study. I knew that many more were to be found in libraries and on friends' floors. How, I thought, would I sift through all this material, and pull out what was best to use. Then I took a simple decision: I decided that where I could write from my own experience or from the experience of groups and communities I knew personally, I would do that. That helped.

Basic Christian communities are not a movement in the church, but the church in movement, as Johannes Metz has said.

This is a helpful thought to bear in mind as you read these stories.

1. Long-Dammed-up Waters

All beginnings are fascinating, and also elusive. Never more so than when one is seeking to trace the first faint puffs of wind that gradually gain momentum and turn suddenly into a gale of some considerable force.

The story of the basic Christian communities (BCCs), or basic ecclesial communities (BECs) as they are also known, is this kind of story. These communities first appeared in Brazil in the 1960s; at least, that is where they were first most apparent. A part of the story, then, can be traced from this point.

In the early 1960s the Second Vatican Council spoke of women and men as "the artisans of a new humanity". This, it told us, was our primary vocation, and the church had one "single intention: that God's kingdom may come". [1]

This was a shift, from a church separate from the world to one fully part of the world and a witness to a new kingdom life-style. It had taken twenty or so years for this shift to happen. The wind had been blowing for some time; it only needed Vatican II to prize open the windows for the wind already gaining strength to do its work.

The shift was not confined to the Catholic Church. It was taking place on a much wider front than that. "The church is that segment of the world which reveals the final goal towards which God is working for the whole world." This statement from the World Council of Churches' document *The Church for Others* (1967) is similar to many statements found in Vatican II documents.

Two world wars had left their scars, but had also contributed to a desperately needed change. If the church was to contribute in any meaningful way to a better world, it would first have to acknowledge itself as part of it — hopefully for the better. And be open to be changed and reshaped by that encounter.

The basic Christian communities were soon to become crucial just at this point — beginning to forge the way ahead — a "new way of being church".

God has made his tent among us

A team of five had come from Brazil to take part in a consultation on international perspectives of rediscovering community.[2] It was in November 1991, at Notre Dame University, USA, that the five told their story to those of us gathered. They told us how the small communities to which they belonged in Sao Paulo had been formed in 1964, after the military coup that had taken place that year. Before that happened, the greater political openness following the overthrow of fascism in 1945 had enabled the growth of popular movements. But this period had come to an abrupt end with the military coup.

With public gatherings and any kind of dissent again banned, the church offered the only alternative — a place to gather, to find support, to plan what to do. And following Vatican II it was a church open to just such opportunity. Small communities began to form, shaped from the beginning by the daily reality of a people living under an oppressive military regime.

Usually accompanied by a priest or a pastorally trained lay person, these communities were made up of about forty persons meeting regularly to pray and reflect on their daily lives in the light of the Bible, and to celebrate their faith. What might at first sight have seemed fairly innocuous was to prove highly explosive.

As the team from Brazil shared their story with us, a large and colourful poster on the wall behind proclaimed: "God has made his tent among us." "This tells us something of our people," they said. "Many have no homes, so they use cloth to make a tent and that is their home. Knowing that God has also set up his tent among us is what gives us the strength to go on."

The majority of those who formed these ecclesial communities at the base were the poor themselves — peasants, labourers, indigenous peoples, the underemployed and unemployed, overcrowded urban-dwellers, young people frustrated by the lack of opportunity for training and work, and old people increasingly marginalized by a progress-oriented society. Now for the first time they were to find they had a voice, and reach the conviction that God was on their side.

In the 1960s the communities were just beginning. By 1974 there were some 40,000; by 1985, 100,000. That was in Brazil alone; it was estimated there were a further 80,000 in other parts of Latin America. In Brazil, as elsewhere, this growth had been helped by diocesan education programmes. The programmes usually took place during Lent, and the themes were chosen in consultation with the communities themselves. Their main objective was the transformation of unjust situations — injustices to do with land, work, the position of women in Brazilian society.

Such diocesan programmes took place in other Latin American countries too. In Chile BECs began in 1963-64 as a result of such a programme conducted mainly in poor urban and rural areas. These were areas far from the already established parish centres, and it was an attempt to make the church present in concrete ways.

BECs came up in a variety of ways. Some formed directly around the desire of a few people to gather to read the scriptures together, others from those who came together to assert a legal right or to struggle for a basic need. Some were formed, as we have seen, as a result of a parish or diocesan programme, or initiated by a priest, nun or lay person who was living among the poor and invited a small group to a scripture reading or to discuss a common problem. The ways are many, but the common element throughout is the drawing together of the social and the religious, of life and faith.

How an individual becomes a member of such a community is illustrated by Manuel's story. In 1973 Chile had experienced a military coup; and the community of which Manuel is a member was formed shortly after that event. At that time Manuel was a nominal Catholic, active in student organizations and protest movements. He had a job in the national health service. After the coup all his outside activities had to come to an end, and he and his wife had little to do but stay at home. It was a strain on their marriage, and Manuel knew he needed to be involved in something, some activity that expressed his concern about what was happening in his country. A neighbour invited him to the small Christian community. It was very different from anything he had experienced before — in the language used, in their way of organizing themselves. There was no voting, every decision was made by consensus. There was no hierarchy. The group broke bread together, reflected on the Bible, and the evening always ended with a cup of tea. It was all strange to him, but it was to make all the difference in his life, and in time in that of his wife as well.

At first his wife would have nothing to do with it, and wanted him to leave the community. Later she relented and went along to the meetings herself. Helped by educational programmes and retreats, they renewed their marriage vows.

This mixture of pastoral and prophetic activity characterizes all the communities.

God's favourites

It was the Peruvian theologian Gustavo Gutiérrez who first reflected in writing on these events. His book, *Theology of Liberation*, published in 1973, caused both delight

and consternation in the northern and southern hemi-
spheres. The term "liberation theology" had been born.
But what was happening in Latin America, Gutiérrez
insisted, was not a new theology, but a new reformation
— a re-formation of the church and its faithfulness to the
God of Jesus Christ.

Events in Latin America followed hard on the heels of
Vatican II. As we have seen, the Council had given
official recognition to a shift already taking place in the
Catholic church. The church had moved from its concern
mainly with a person's soul to a concern with the whole
person, from an emphasis on the inherent evil in human-
kind to seeing women and men as the artisans of a new
humanity. It was now emphasizing the place and gifts of
all Christians as "the new people of God". From a reluc-
tant recognition of the need for some adaptation to other
cultures, the church was now speaking about God being
present in other cultures.

The thinking of Vatican II in these and other areas was
to go even further in the years that followed, but in 1962
the "long-dammed-up waters" began to flow. And in the
words of Gustavo Gutiérrez, the floodgates that had held
back these waters for so long were opened up in Latin
America at Medellín, Colombia.[3] That was in 1968, six
years after the start of the Vatican Council.

Medellín was where the second Latin American
Bishops' Conference met. The first had met at Rio de
Janeiro in 1955. "The Church in the Current Transformation of Latin America in the Light of Vatican II" was the
theme at Medellín. In the years since 1955 the Latin
American church had begun to come of age, taken a fresh
look at the situation in which it found itself and started a
search for new and appropriate ways to respond to what it
perceived — as a bearer of the good news of Jesus Christ.

What became clear to many of the bishops who were
at Medellín was that the principal cause of the poverty in

which the majority of their people lived was an external one — the capitalist economic system that led invariably to wealth for a few and poverty for the rest. Internally wealthy oligarchies were kept in power to serve the economic interests of Western powers. It was a situation that led again and again throughout Latin America to "institutionalized violence" — the violence of poverty, injustice, alienation and exploitation that took no account of every person's right to dignity of life. This was a gospel matter. The Medellín documents called the church to a "preferential option for the poor". Only that way could the church have integrity and proclaim the good news.

This issue of the challenge of poverty was again taken up at the third Latin American Bishops' Conference convened ten years later at Puebla, Mexico, in 1979. The action that the church had initiated during the decade had resulted in its becoming the focus of controversy, and led to much persecution. There were many church leaders who were now opposed to the position the conference at Medellín had taken. Despite this opposition, the "preferential option for the poor" was made even more integral to the church's life in the final documents of the Puebla meeting. What was meant by "institutionalized injustice" was now made even more explicit. It implied two clear tendencies: "a thrust towards modernization, entailing strong economic growth", and "the tendency... towards pauperization and growing exclusion of the vast majority of Latin Americans from production". Here the church was taking on not only the power of the oligarchies but the presence of multinational corporations in Latin America. Further, Puebla coined its own condemnatory phrase: "social sinfulness". The situation was all the more serious because it existed in countries that called themselves Catholic. There could be no good news if this situation of sin was not addressed.

Pope John Paul II said, speaking in a poor neighbour-hood of the city of Guadalajara in Mexico:

> I have earnestly desired this meeting because I feel solidar-ity with you, and because you, being poor, have the right to my special concern and attention. I will tell you the reason: the pope loves you because you are God's favourites. In founding his family, the church, God had in mind poor and needy humanity. To redeem it, he sent his Son specifically who was born poor and lived among the poor to make us rich with his poverty. [4]

It was against this background that the BECs con-tinued to grow. The proclamation of the good news was already happening in a new way. In the ten years since Medellín the communities had multiplied and matured throughout Latin America. Now at Puebla they were referred to as a cause "for joy and hope in the church. In the communion with their bishops, and in line with Medellín's request, they have become centres of evangelization and moving forces for liberation and development. The vitality of the BECs is now beginning to bear fruit." [5]

Lay people exercise their rights

The year the Latin American bishops gathered at Medellín — 1968 — was also a momentous year in Europe. Here too was revolt, students rioting on the streets of Paris and other major European cities. Not only students, but academics, workers and many hundreds of ordinary people saying they had had enough of hierarchy, of oppression, of injustice.

A number of basic Christian communities (BCCs) in Europe were born at this time. For many progressive Catholics Vatican II was an affirmation of the beliefs they already held. To others it came as a new understanding of themselves as the people of God, living and working in the world, helping to create a more humane and just society. Priests, religious, lay, they took to the streets in large numbers, seeking just this. Friendships were formed, and that was one way the first small communities came into being.

But if these mass movements of the late 1960s and early 1970s were a fertile ground for the growth of many of these first European BCCs, the seed had been dormant in the ground for some time. A number of communities, particularly in France, see their origins going further back, tracing them to the worker-priest movement that began in Paris in the 1940s, first as an "experiment" to send priests to work in the factories and dockyards. It was a bold undertaking on the part of the then archbishop of Paris, Cardinal Suhard, and one that made him the centre of considerable controversy. The worker-priest movement grew and had an influence far beyond its immediate concerns, not least in helping to form the thinking of Pope John XXIII — the pope of the Council. The movement was aligned with a number of radical movements that came into being in the 1930s and 1940s. The "see, judge, act" methodology that is now a foundational educational tool used in basic Christian communities worldwide was first devised and used by the Catholic Workers Movement that began in France in the 1930s.

Now in the 1960s in many parts of Europe the struggle was not only against the authoritarianism of the state, but also against that of the church. Often it was a protest against the connivance of the church in the social and economic policies of the political party in power. In September 1968 a group of Italian students occupied the cathedral in Parma to make just such a protest — against the involvement of church authorities in economic and political power structures and the persistent denial to lay people of their rights within the church. The ruling church body (the curia) called in the police and the young people were ejected.

When the nearby parish community of Isoletto sent an open letter of encouragement to the young people, they were immediately asked by the archbishop of Florence to withdraw their support. A tussle ensued. The letter had been sent not by the priest himself but by the whole parish community. The bishop refused to speak to the community, and insisted on dealing only with the priest. He was not allowed to have his way.

In the story of BCCs in Italy this is spoken of as "foundational". That a community of believers should consider it their right to dialogue with the bishop was "a disturbing departure from common ecclesiastical practice". But it was a growth point for the communities themselves.

Out of just such stormy waters, a number of Italian communities were born. The beginning of the parish community of Isoletto itself is an example.

Fr Erno Mazzi, the parish priest, had been engaged in church and social reform since the early 1950s, and had been reproved by the local bishop for his innovative activities. The Isoletto community's support for the students' occupation of Parma cathedral led to legal action being taken against Fr Mazzi, and the community was forced to vacate the parish church. The community finally opted to do so peacefully, but to continue to be present as a believing church by celebrating the eucharist every Sunday in the central square — whatever the weather! When in 1985 I visited the community, they were still continuing this practice.

The act of the students in occupying the cathedral had been condemned by the pope. Already by 1968 the Vatican had become uneasy about these communities. This in itself helped to hasten the growth of the BCCs in Europe, for increasingly they became the one place where progressive Catholics could find a home.

Inspiration to go on

It was not only in predominantly Catholic countries that the communities grew. In the Netherlands many communities came into being in the 1970s and 1980s. Ekklesia in The Hague is one of them.

"Help rid the world of nuclear weapons. Let it begin in the Netherlands" was the slogan of Holland's peace movement in the 1970s. During the annual Peace Week a million or more people poured into the streets of The Hague to pressurize the Dutch government not to accept cruise missiles on Dutch soil.

The Dutch churches, Protestant and Catholic, gave their support to this movement, as in the 1960s they had given a lead in helping to raise awareness about human rights and aid for third-world countries. And as in the student protests in France, friendships were formed — on the streets. Those who found they had shared beliefs soon began to say to each other: "What are are we doing? We are together as Christians Monday to Friday, concerned about the same things, and on Sundays we go our different ways. Wouldn't it make more sense if we were together on Sundays too?"

Lay people, Protestant pastors, Catholic religious and priests were all asking the same questions. "Why not form a Sunday congregation?" a priest suggested. A letter was sent out, people responded, and the first official celebration of Ekklesia Den Haag took place on 10 March 1974.

A friend and I visited the community in 1989. We took part in their Sunday worship, that Sunday led by young people, members of the community. The young people were taking their turn; they did not want to be patronized: "No applause, please, just because we are young people." We met in a large room in a disused chapel in a poor neighbourhood, simply furnished, the walls decorated with colourful posters, some done by the children and young people, and others brought back from various demonstrations. A large cross at the centre, immensely striking, with the black figure of a Salvadorean peasant portraying Jesus. This is also used in demonstrations, especially at the annual commemoration of the assassination of Archbishop Oscar Romero of El Salvador in March 1980.

Sunday is the only time during the week when all members come together, but there are other occasions when members meet in smaller groups — three women's groups, a theology group, and monthly meetings of small groups for family meals. There may also be shared tasks, but more often it will be as members of other justice and peace groups that members of the community meet one another — "... and on Sunday you find the inspiration to continue," is how one member put it. While at Ekklesia my friend and I took part in two peace demonstrations, both protests against nuclear weapons.

Ekklesia has a written constitution, but that is not often referred to. Such formalities are held to lightly. I read through it and liked it. Part of it reads, "... following Jesus Messiah, striving for justice and peace, we hope to be part of the people of God on their way... to become a sign of the messianic community in a modest but still a real way." The modest part is important to them; that year they had taken as a theme for reflection and action: "Don't try to have high ideals, but first look where you are, what you do and what the outcome is."[6]

12

NOTES

[1] Vatican II, Pastoral Constitution on the Church in the Modern World (*Gaudium et Spes*), para.45.

[2] "Rediscovering Community: International Perspectives", an international consultation on basic Christian communities held at the University of Notre Dame, Indiana, USA, in 1991. This consultation, sponsored by the Institute for Pastoral and Social Ministry at Notre Dame University, is referred to a number of times in this book.

[3] Gustavo Gutiérrez, *The Power of the Poor in History*, London, SCM, 1983, p.34.

[4] *Ibid.*, p. 138.

[5] Extract from the conclusions of the Latin American Bishops' Conference held at Puebla, Mexico, in January 1979, cited in *ibid*.

[6] The story of Ekklesia was first told in *Communities* by Jeanne Hinton, published by Eagle, Guildford, UK, 1993.

2. Creating One's Own History

The growth of the grassroots communities in Latin America was soon to be repeated in the Philippines. Medellín was to be an important influence here as elsewhere. The news of what was happening in Latin America was spreading, and missionaries in Mindanao and the Visayas in the Philippines, inspired by the concept and growth of basic ecclesial communities in Latin America, established the first basic Christian communities in these regions in the late 1960s.

In 1971 a conference on "Building Basic Christian Communities" was convened by the Mindanao-Sulu Pastoral Conference. It inspired other dioceses to implement similar programmes. In 1972 martial law was declared, and as in many Latin American countries this was to spur the growth of the communities. A number of dioceses began to implement the programme of building BCCs, and the Catholic Bishops' Conference of the Philippines gave it official sanction.

It took time, but gradually under the pressure of circumstances these communities moved from purely liturgical activities to engagement first in social welfare programmes and then in community development projects. A more important step needed to be taken, that of moving to community organizing. Only at this point did the BCCs become identified with the mass of the Filipino people, who were already organizing to liberate themselves and to create their own future. By taking this step, however, the communities found they had lost the approval of the official church. It did not take long for that to happen.

Taking root and touching the ground

Mass protests in the late 1960s and early 1970s had been condemned by the church. There were protests against military bases on Philippine soil, against economic inequities, against the erosion of cultural identity and against human-rights abuses. The rallies, the church thought, threatened order and stability. Not all church persons responded this way. Some saw the potential for needed social change, and applauded the move of the Filipino people to "create their own history". They began to work alongside the people.

In 1976 the initials BCC were changed to BCC-CO. This marked a fundamental change — "the formation of basic Christian communities through the application of the principles of community organizing". Gradually the worsening economic situation and the inadequacy of development programmes to meet the need for social change moved others to the same stance. The critical questions in evaluating any action were "for whom?" and "with whom?". For community leaders the priority had become very clear: they should serve, first of all, not the institutional church, but the poor, the deprived and the oppressed.

The experience of one community organizer is revealing:

> We organized the community for some eight months. During this period, there were leaders who emerged. But there were several shifts and changes in the centre of leadership, just as there were in our thrusts. We started organizing on community issues, like filling materials and electrical services, when we should have begun with the problems of the fish haulers *(batilyos)*. When we did go into organizing the *batilyos*, they provided the centre or leadership and more or less stabilized our organized work in the areas. If we had started by organizing the *batilyos* rather than the whole community, organizing would have been faster. [1]

This change of direction, however, was increasingly to bring persecution as injustices and brutality were exposed. Many community members were to die as martyrs for their actions. In the process, though, a new way of being church was emerging. This was happening as the church tried "to 'take root and touch the ground' by entering into the world of the poor and creating possibilities for the poor to become, in reality, the *church*." [2]

A medical missionary sister who had served in the Philippines but was away for ten years returned in the early 1980s and was present at an assembly convened by the Roman Catholic diocese of Ipil. About 120 persons, ordained and lay, were present. What she saw amazed her:

> When I left these people would have been cowed and voiceless in any assembly of this kind. They would have accepted that it was their superiors who had the right to tell them what to do and think, and they would not have dared raise a word in protest. But what have we here? Bishop Escaler is not even taking the chair — it is a young layman who guides the assembly, with the bishop contributing from time to time with the others. Women with families, fishermen, landless labourers, young people are making thoughtful and articulate contributions. They listen carefully to others and take their own share in trying to discern the will of God for the diocese. And their sense of dignity before God, their confidence, their determination — all spring from their faith! Many times they are afraid, as they experience the violence and destructiveness which they meet in daily experience. But they stand, and they stand together. [3]

Incarnated in a people and a culture

In other parts of Asia BCCs are not so well developed, indeed in some parts hardly at all. About half of all Asian Christians live in the Philippines, so this is hardly surprising. In total only three and a half percent of Asia's population is Christian.

Since Christians are only a small minority, the need for BCCs is not immediately apparent, numerically at least. Most Christians in a given area already know and interact with each other. Other factors, however, have put BCCs on the Asian church's agenda.

Asia's religious crisis is one such factor. Delegates at an Asian colloquium on "Ministries of the Church" held in Hong Kong in 1977 concluded that the most promising solution to this crisis lay in BCCs. A minority church — considered by many as imported and undesirable, a "wholly foreign religion", identified with colonial rule and still carrying much of its symbolism and trappings — was indeed in need of change. The conference concluded that BCCs were to be promoted because in the Asian context "the individual Christian can best survive, grow and develop as a Christian person in the midst of a self-nourishing, self-governing, self-ministering and self-propagating Christian community".

Two years later in Manila, in 1979, an international congress on mission made a more explicit statement. The church in Asia needed to become "genuinely local... incarnated in a people and a culture, in a particular time and place". This localization and concretization of the church found expression in BCCs, the conference concluded. Their emergence everywhere spoke of a need that is being met — the people's need "to express real interpersonal relationships and feel a sense of communal belonging, and where they can assume more and more the responsibility they have for the church".

In India, despite the strong recommendations of Asian church leaders, the development of BCCs has been slow. More than recommendations is needed, reflects Joseph Prasad Pinto, a Capuchin priest from Mangalore; there has to be an ongoing commitment to help facilitate the emergence of BCCs. Besides, he writes, clericalism is deeply rooted in India's "ancient churches" and acts as a brake on lay initiatives.[4]

Pinto sees a number of similarities among the many liberation groups that have arisen in India in recent years, groups working to bring about socio-political change and liberate people from oppression and exploitation. Christians are active in some of these liberation movements, gathering together to support and encourage one another, to read the Bible together and to celebrate the eucharist. They are involved because they believe in the necessity of working at the grassroots if any liberation movement is to be effective. In just such a way BCCs have emerged in Europe, the USA, Australia and other parts of the world.

Pinto gives an example of such a group in Bombay Central. Here a Jesuit priest, Paul Vaz, has brought together a team to encourage and enable local people to campaign for basic necessities: water, food, electricity and sanitary facilities. In this area, the Bellasis Chawls, twenty two-storeyed buildings are each home to eighty families. On average ten people live in each house which consists only of a single room, sharing common toilets. In these squalid blocks some 10,000 people struggle to survive; the majority are Hindus, with small concentrations of Christians, Neo-Buddhists and Muslims.

Improvements have come about through the action taken by small groups. Most active in them are the women and the youth. The men, at work during the day, have less time to give; the women have greater influence in the bringing up of the family, and are more responsive to the idea of campaigning for a better future. In addition to improved conditions, other positive results are apparent: "... a sense of community, respect for other communities of faith, interest in dialogue with members of other communities of faiths, a sense of service to the community".

In addition to this, Christians in the Chawls have formed their own BCCs, and now gather to read the Bible and celebrate the eucharist together. They do this always conscious of their own immediate situation. A genuinely local development.

**No Christian without a group,
no group without a Christian**

In the early 1990s a Chinese sister who had worked with the basic Christian communities in the Philippines moved to Taiwan to help in the formation of similar grassroots communities there.

The development of Christian faith communities (CFCs), as they are called in Taiwan, began in the late 1980s with a week-long symposium on evangelization. To form at least one CFC in every (Catholic) parish was one of the important resolutions made there. This was followed up by an open letter written by the Catholic bishops encouraging its implementation. Help was sought from a number of organizations that could provide animators, Legion of Mary, Cursillo, and Volunteer Lay Apostles among them.

The development of CFCs among Catholics in Taiwan is seen as crucial to evangelization. Parishes are too big for any sense of community to grow. And this at a time when traditional kinship or friendship groups are breaking down because of increased mobility, and there is a search for new forms of bonding.

Not all the communities are parish-based. One meets in a bank; its members come from that bank and two others. The communities have a slogan: "No Christian without a group, no group without a Christian." Their aims are to build a sense of community, to reflect on faith and daily life, to celebrate faith, and to act together. Action may be responding to the needs of the faith community or its members, or to needs encountered at work or in the neighbourhoods where members live.

The change of name from basic Christian communities to Christian faith communities has its own story. Some bishops did not want the communities to be identified too closely with the basic ecclesial communities in Latin America, and asked them to choose another name for themselves; they chose Christian faith communities. However, they see themselves as definitely "counter-cultural", ready to question and press for social change where called for. There are small Protestant groups that are in some ways similar, but in the experience of the Christian faith communities these are more likely to affirm rather than question the status quo. The CFCs of Taiwan identify themselves with the worldwide network of grassroots communities that are committed to challenge whatever they perceive as opposed to the kingdom vision of God's reign of justice and peace.

There is also another purpose behind the development of the Christian faith communities in Taiwan — that of establishing authentically Chinese communities which would be able at the right time to share their story with Christians in mainland China. [5]

That Christians in the People's Republic of China used to gather secretly in small house churches is well known (some of their stories are told in Raymond Fung's *Households of God on China's Soil*[6]). Many of these small Christian communities would probably embrace the orientation and values of BCCs in other parts of the world. They have not, however, had the advantage of being able to learn first-hand of the existence and witness of those outside China. Likewise, there has been little or no contact with them from groups elsewhere. The situation is comparable to that between Eastern and Western Europe before the collapse of the iron curtain — a situation that has now altered to the advantage of BCCs on both sides.

Simply being with the poor

Hong Kong also is preparing for change. May 1989 marked a new stepping-off point for the Catholic diocese: its pastoral policy was outlined in a paper bravely entitled "March into the Bright Decade". In 1997 China will recover sovereignty over Hong Kong and, with this in mind, the formation of basic Christian communities was presented as urgent and essential. A three-year project was started to help with the formation of small faith communities (SFCs). It was to be led by the Catholic Institute for Religion and Society.

The Institute does not see SFCs as a new model of the church, but as "church at the grassroots level, a living cell, a complete unit. It is the most practical expression of the presence of the church in society." It could be of tremendous help in a situation where the church might have to face persecution or adversity. Those who prepared the original paper considered that parishes and church buildings in prominent places were far too obvious to be safe places to gather.

In other parts of Asia, too, basic Christian communities or small faith communities are growing. In Singapore the development of housing estates has encouraged the growth of these "neighbourhood groups" or "home churches". They are often made up of families or individuals living on different levels of an apartment block. In rural areas of East Malaysia villagers come together in units, the various units making up one large parish. In Sri Lanka parishes are likewise beginning to break down into cottage groups, prayer groups or BCCs. In Indonesia village motivators work with the rural poor to help bring about a new awareness of their situation and the means to respond to it concretely. These motivators come from the churches and work in small teams. In South Korea a number of new "messianic communities" or "congregations" came into being in 1974, following a wave of arrests and detention of political dissidents. Christians were imprisoned for protesting about the conditions of the poor. At the heart of this resistance was a weekly "prayer meeting", which drew many hundreds of people once the detentions started, and to which Buddhists and people of other religions also came. From those who came to pray small communities grew, such as "Peace Market", "House of Dawn", "The Spirit of March 1", "Group of 18" (a women's group) — evocative names that tell their own stories. "We are with the poor. We are therefore ready to go to prison any time," they say.

These different types of small communities or groups that have emerged in Asia all have a similar motivation: they have grown in response to a particular call or initiative. A church that is close to people inevitably becomes close also to those of other faiths. People learn to share their material and spiritual resources. It is thus a way of building interfaith communities as well.

"What does it mean to be the church of the poor?" asked Bishop Julio X. Labayen of the Philippines in a paper presented at the 25th anniversary of the Dutch bishops' Lenten action. "Isn't the church for all men and women, for rich and poor, for saints and sinners?"

> We found an answer in the way many of the churches of Asia are moving in the direction of greater and greater involvement with the life of their people: their simply being with the poor; their attempts at working out programmes of human development — integral, respectful of the people's dignity, attuned to their cultures; their standing with them in their hard struggle for justice and for self-empowerment. They insist that the rich become themselves real members of the church of the poor, by fulfilling their obligations in justice and charity towards the poor.

"Come down to the people"

Evangelization was also a concern of the Catholic bishops in East Africa.

In December 1973, a gathering of the Association of the Member Episcopal Conferences of Eastern Africa was convened to plan for the East African church into the 1980s. The problem they faced was that to most ordinary Africans the church had little or no relevance. Indeed, they concluded that the Catholic Church really had no future in Eastern Africa — unless it discovered a way "to come down to the people". The only way they could see this happening was through the church shaping itself into small grassroots communities. "If this is the case, let us be the small communities," they said.

From that point on the East African bishops took it as a pastoral priority to work towards each diocese becoming a "community of communities", and programmes were initiated to bring this about. In the Rulenge diocese in Tanzania this work had already begun, but it became apparent that it takes more than a diocesan programme to bring it about.

Parishes in Rulenge had been divided into small Christian communities, formation programmes followed, and the Bible was being studied, but the bishop, Christopher Mwoleka, knew that a vital element was missing. In most places there was little integration with the wider community and its needs; the church had not yet "come down to the people". In 1983 a diocesan team was formed to encourage parishes and communities to move in this direction, but the results were still meagre. It was then that Bishop Mwoleka concluded that growth would only come about if the diocesan teams were themselves modelled on the kind of community they had in mind.

"I will be the first to put my life on the line," he said, "but I need others of you to join me." Sixteen persons, including four families, agreed to do so. The bishop himself moved out to live in the small rural parish of Bushangaro. Those who had property sold it, and with this capital they started their life together. Within seven years the community had grown to three hundred, extending over three parishes.

Christopher Mwoleka was present at the 1991 Notre Dame consultation.

We share everything in common, we bring up our children together, we attend to the sick and elderly together. We grow bananas, keep cows and pigs and "live by our own sweat". Many of our members are unskilled, but we try to help young men acquire skills: carpentry, brick-laying, farming. We try to help each person to get work to meet his or her needs and also those of others in the community. We aim to be self-reliant but that is not the main purpose. The main purpose is to gain strength to serve in the wider community. We run some local shops that sell goods at the lowest possible prices to help the local community.

This "integrated community", as it is called, has a particular evangelistic task — to inspire and help in the formation of small Christian communities (SCCs). Other SCCs, however, are likely to form themselves around more everyday concerns. Typically a community comes together only once a week, meeting informally in the homes of members.

There are five such "neighbourhood small Christian communities" in the Geita diocese in Tanzania. The host family prepares each week's Bible reading. Women are in the majority, and this means that Bible-sharing usually focuses on their life situations: the role of women in society, human rights, and liberation in situations of marginalization.

The gospel story of Mary Magdalene meeting the risen Jesus was the Bible passage for a group meeting during the 1994 International Year of the Family. To see Mary as the model of a liberated woman was encouraging to those present. "Despite many difficulties, women should use their will power to develop their talents. Women should liberate themselves," one woman concluded. The group discussed her statement, and agreed that the problems facing women today should be tackled seriously by women themselves. This could be best done, they concluded, through Christian social analysis and through making use of the media.

At the end of each week's Bible sharing they would decide on a specific action they should take up. One week they decided that, just as Mary Magdalene was a messenger to Peter and John and the other disciples, so also they should go to their husbands and persuade them to build up the SCCs. [7]

"We are the church"

While the development of small Christian communities is strongest in East Africa, parts of West Africa were not far behind. Martin George is a young Catholic layman from Freetown, Sierra Leone, a catechist and an animator of SCCs. I met him at Notre Dame in 1991. He emphasized the importance of the small Christian community. His own community, made up of adults and young people, meets once a week "to share needs, joys and sorrows". The meetings are usually held in the open, often in front of a member's house, or in a sitting room. As in all SCCs, regular reflection on a Bible passage plays an important role. "The Seven Steps" is the form Bible reflection usually takes. These are:

1) opening prayer;
2) reading the text;
3) picking out words or short phrases, reading them aloud prayerfully, and keeping silence in between;
4) keeping a period of silence; allowing God to speak;
5) sharing what each has heard;
6) discussing any tasks the group commits itself to do;
7) concluding with a prayer and a hymn.

It is important, Martin said, that they are looking for real answers to social questions. There are various ways of responding to social needs: youth programmes, care for the sick, the elderly and the marginalized, support for small cooperatives and developing ways to work collectively in planting, harvesting and other tasks.

A T-shirt produced by the communities bears an important message: "We are the church." One of the biggest problems encountered by those encouraging the formation of SCCs was that it was not the way most Catholics perceived themselves. "Church" meant the building, or the priest, not ordinary people like themselves. For Martin this has been one of the most destructive and pervasive legacies of colonialism, totally opposed to the African's innate sense of his or her own place in the natural community. "We are the church" T-shirts were distributed all over West Africa. The message gradually began to change people's perceptions.

In the 1970s the growth of SCCs in other parts of Africa was slow. Nevertheless, the effectiveness of basic Christian communities impressed the Swiss theologian Walbert Bühlmann when he visited South Africa in 1979. The best way to promote the gospel, he asserted, was by means of such communities. He gave as examples those that had sprung up in Angola and Mozambique "in spite of — or because of — the fact that Marxists had taken control of many church institutions".

Bühlmann was answering questions put to him by Marjorie Hope and James Young, co-authors of *The South African Churches in a Revolutionary Situation*. The two authors also asked a young black priest, Lebamang Sebidi: "And how do you see the future of Catholicism?"

> Basic communities! That's the church of tomorrow! Right now the form and rules of the church come from Rome, which is only a political structure. What do we need? Not conglomerations of individuals like the "congregation" at Regina Mundi [the large Catholic church in Soweto], but smaller groups of individuals whom we can call by name. We need spontaneity and latitude for incorporating African traditions.

While small Christian communities have not yet developed to any great extent in South Africa, it is there that many of the materials used to help form communities in Africa and beyond originate. The Lumko Missiological Institute, itself a small Christian community that promotes gospel neighbourhood groups, produces educational materials used by basic Christian communities throughout the world. One of the most moving moments at the Notre Dame consultation came during the presentation given by the team from Taiwan. As a part of this presentation they showed their teaching aids, using an overhead projector. When the first picture appeared on the screen there was a spontaneous outburst of delighted recognition from the Africans present. The Asians were using the Lumko Institute teaching aids, in an adapted form. Asian faces and dress had replaced African, and headings were in Chinese characters, but the teaching point was the same. It was "a profound moment", as many said later, capturing in a significant way the sense of being together on the same journey.

Needed — a change of mentality

One of the problems encountered by those engaged in the promotion of SCCs on the African continent is that their growth has been less spontaneous than, for instance, in Latin America. The African bishops met, saw the need, and planned how it could happen. "It was not really the need felt from below which gave rise to them," Bishop Patrick Kalilombe was to point out later. He said that there may be the danger that "the building of communities is in the heads of the bishops and perhaps not in the people's mind". He added, however, that he had the strong feeling that unforeseen developments were bound to follow. "I know that we have not fully reflected on all it means to put the church in the hands of the laity."

Jac Hedsen and James Holme-Siedle worked for seven years in a parish in eastern Uganda and found they had varied success in forming communities. In 1980 they spent three months visiting basic Christian communities in Chile and Brazil and learning from them. There the importance of conversion, of a changed attitude, became real to them.

> The first requirement for the establishment of BCCs seems to be a very fundamental one: namely, the need for a change of attitude or mentality on the part of all who are involved in this new pastoral policy. A change of pastoral structures remains without result if it is not accompanied by a change of mentality, a conversion, one could call it. Embarking on building up BCCs means looking at the church in a different light. It means becoming aware of the fact that the church means first of all the people, the faithful... This pastoral policy requires that the church be looked at from the grassroots rather than from the top. [8]

In Africa the small Christian communities did not, with some exceptions, suffer persecution, unlike their counterparts in Latin America. Most of the communities had not been born in a revolutionary situation. Their problems were different, though acute. Growth in most parts has been slower. Except in East Africa.

"Is this development linked to that in Latin America and Asia?", Patrick Kalilombe was asked. He answered that his own thinking about basic Christian communities had been stimulated by his knowledge of the communities in Latin America and that it continued to be fed by them. He concluded:

> I think it's a general movement which is penetrating insensibly and is being communicated all over the church. Even in Europe and America where you would feel that this is not happening, it certainly is happening much more than we think, but in other forms. [9]

NOTES

[1] *Moving Heaven and Earth*, Commission on the Churches' Participation in Development, Manila, 1982.

[2] BCC-CO leaflet, *Towards a New Way of Being Church*.

[3] Margaret and Ian Fraser, *Wind and Fire*, Dunblane, Basic Communities Resource Centre, 1986.

[4] Joseph Prasad Pinto, OFM, *Inculturation through Basic Communities: An Indian Perspective*, Bangalore, Asian Trading Corporation, 1985.

[5] As shared by Sr Victorina D. Palanca at Notre Dame in 1991.

[6] Geneva, WCC, 1982.

[7] Story told by Sr Rita Ishengoma from Geita, Tanzania, in *International Papers on Pastoral Ministry*, August-September 1994. Published quarterly by University of Notre Dame, Indiana, USA.

[8] *Spearhead*, published by AMECEA Gaba, Eldoret, Kenya, no. 75.

[9] In an interview with Ian Fraser.

3. How Can We Build a People of Hope?

Are basic Christian communities transferable? From South to North, from the third world to the industrialized world? "Not directly transferable," concluded a report published in Britain in 1989. Despite the fact that this was a qualified "no", this statement from the *Faith in the City* report was heatedly debated both immediately following its publication and ever since. That is an indication of the interest in basic Christian communities. Indeed the report, commissioned by the archbishop of Canterbury in the wake of race riots in several major British cities, recommended "the development of centres, preferably ecumenical, in each neighbourhood (for example in house groups) which reach out in care and concern for the whole life of the neighbourhood and all its peoples. Small groups for prayer, Bible study, healing, and theological reflection on local issues would be based on them."[1]

Not unlike BCCs, after all. Nevertheless, *Faith in the City* had concluded that Latin America's model of basic Christian communities was not directly transferable because they were "peasant and pre-industrial, not concerned with upward social mobility" and with "little reliance on outside professionals". Whether such statements are true or not, one difficulty in assessing the growth and influence of basic Christian communities in Britain is the complexity of the situation.

Sowing the seeds

The early 1970s saw the rapid growth of a number of Christian communities, some large, some small, many of them coming out of the charismatic renewal that was at its peak in the 1970s (my own community, of which I am a Companion, was founded in these years). David Clark, a Methodist minister and a college lecturer in community and youth work, aware of this phenomenon, established in 1981 a National Centre for Christian Communities and

Networks, convened annual gatherings, and started a quarterly publication called *Community*. But were the members really basic Christian communities? Others who held to a strictly urban or more radical agenda questioned this. They believed such communities had a role but, mainly white and middle-class, they were unlikely to further the growth of a distinctly British liberation theology or reach the British working classes. (Many of these communities had only a brief life; they ceased to exist within ten years. The networks, on the other hand, have grown and proliferated, many concerned with urban questions and with justice and peace issues.)

While the debate about what is a basic Christian community in the British context has continued, other reports also had their points to make. At its national pastoral congress in 1980 the Roman Catholic Church of England and Wales had "overwhelmingly recommended that parishes should become a communion of Christian communities incorporating small, neighbourhood, area and special interest groups". [2]

Three years later, an Anglican report on the church's ministry (known widely as the Tiller report, after the chairperson, Canon John Tiller, then chief secretary of the advisory council for the church's ministry of the Church of England) advocated far-reaching and revolutionary changes. It suggested replacing parish priests responsible for the overall life of a parish with diocesan and deanery ministry teams giving support and direction to a variety of cells or groups of lay people, sometimes retaining the parish structures and sometimes not. Such cells, the report envisaged, could be house groups within a parish, or those involved in community projects, in work with down-and-outs, in housing associations, in running bookshops. Some would be prayer groups, others could be formed in industry, commerce, education, medicine and government. [3]

Again, all of this is essentially a plea for something very like basic Christian communities as found in Latin America or elsewhere in the world. And meanwhile developments were taking place on the ground. One was in an inner-city area in Glasgow. In 1980 the Catholic parish of Our Lady and St George, Penilee, began a ten-year programme to transform the parish into "a community of communities". The programme was initiated by the Catholic renewal group, Movement for a Better World, which has helped in the formation of BCCs worldwide. One parishioner looks back to 1980 and shudders at what she remembers: "Those at the centre doing everything and masses of people doing nothing."

The "Tomorrow's Parish" programme started with a parish retreat. Two hundred parishioners came and together they dreamed. The dream was of "a living Christian community, witnessing to the values of Jesus and empowered to build his kingdom of justice, peace and joy". Concretely they saw this happening through the growth of "small dynamic communities". By 1985, neighbourhood groups (as they came to be called) were established. A typical gathering of such a group is a time of discussion based on a scripture reading, followed by further discussion on how the reading applies to the everyday life of group members, to the welfare of the neighbourhood and to wider society. A period of prayer is followed by a decision on some common action the members could take. The set readings and the form of the meeting are only meant as a guide. An urgent concern may take over at some points. One group, concerned by how little contact neighbours had with one another, organized street barbecues, set up a neighbourhood watch scheme and started to raise funds for a nearby children's hospital, all of which helped to bring the neighbours together.

It meant a new attitude and response not just from the lay members, but from the parish priests too. One assistant priest, writing about the feeling many priests have that lay members lack the experience to be fully involved in pastoral planning, commented that there is too often a tendency "to underestimate the depth of commonsense which most lay people have had to develop and apply to a whole variety of different areas of life, including their faith!"

Faith in the City did make an impact in a number of areas and helped to bring in funding for projects that continue to aid the church in large cities. *The Easter People*, the report of the 1980 national pastoral congress, helped to bring about some development of the kind it envisaged, particularly in the Arundel and Brighton diocese, where a formation programme for small Christian communities was started the following year. The Tiller report, on the other hand, fell flat on its face. Not for lack of vision but, it would seem, because it was too visionary.

Too visionary, that is, for the general synod of the Anglican Church. There was to be no pastoral plan here to help in the formation of BCCs as in Brazil, the Philippines or East Africa. What there has been, however, is the encouragement and skills of a team that has returned over a number of years to Britain to facilitate the emergence of BCCs here. The team consists of two Sisters, Carolee Chanona from Belize and Teolide Trevisan from Brazil, and Father José Marins, an adviser to the Brazilian Bishops' Conference, who was also one of the theological experts at Medellín in 1968 and a facilitator at Puebla in 1979. The workshop, which the team has taken to many parts of the world, is usually called "A New Way of Being Church", but is more often known as the Marins workshop. They come not with some ideal model in mind, but to sow "seeds" which they encourage participants to take back home and sow in their own locations.

For many years it was to Birmingham that the team came to run workshops, sponsored by the Saltley Trust and by CAFOD (Catholic Fund for Overseas Development). In the 1980s a £160 million complex had been built close to Birmingham's city centre. This was the International Convention Centre (ICC), a dream come true for the city council. They predicted the complex would attract "wealth and fortune on a scale never seen before". The money, they said, would bring about the regeneration of whole areas of the city that were poor and run down. The ICC was put up in just such an area, Ladywood. Council tower blocks sat alongside the new centre, and were considered an eye-sore by many. The residents of the estate were anxious; they didn't believe in "the dream", only feared its consequences for them.

In the mid-1980s a group of Christians associated with a number of different local congregations became disturbed about the situation. Most lived or worked in or near the estate. They too were sceptical of the council's promises of regeneration, and concerned for the people of Ladywood whose interests they knew were not being represented. Over the telephone, at the end of meetings and on street corners they talked about the situation. One result was that in 1988 they helped to form the Ladywood community forum to give the people of Ladywood a voice.

For at least one member, Jan, an important question had been raised: "What does it mean to be the church here at Ladywood?" It was at this point that the Marins workshop played a crucial part. Jan and eleven others attended the workshop; three questions emerged as a result.

How can we build a people of hope?

How can we get the people of Ladywood together in a meaningful, Christ-centred way?

What are the signs of hope in Ladywood? Is a group of committed radical Christians one of them?

Out of this process of reflection and action a community was born with the aim of being "a visible loving

Christian community of openness, reflection and celebration". The community has a base, a small flat in one of the tower blocks. In September 1991 two sisters came to live in the flat, to provide space — "reflection space, celebration space, hospitality space" — for all those who want to be part of the work of Doorway.[4]

The story of Doorway is but one of the many initiatives emerging from the "seeds" sown by José, Carolee and Teo. Those who attend these workshops come from all walks of life, from all denominations and from all parts of Britain. In more recent years the team has begun to travel to different parts of Britain and Ireland to encourage nascent groups and communities where they are. More and more they are able to be in the background as "encouragers". An ongoing formation course has also been established at a mission college in Birmingham, the course building on insights brought to Britain by the Brazilian team. Other initiatives are emerging from this.

In 1990 I began a research project to see what kind of Christian base groups or communities were emerging in Britain and Ireland. They were to be found at all levels — in urban and rural neighbourhoods, in parishes, dioceses and even church organizations. These organizations were looking for a new way of working together as Christian people, the inspiration for this drawn from basic Christian communities. There were many networks of small groups scattered across the country, most often engaged in justice and peace work of various kinds, others of a more contemplative nature. The Catholic justice and peace groups are an example of the former. Those who form these groups in Catholic parishes throughout the country engage in tasks that anyone can do — "letter writing, prayer, petitions, vigils, raising awareness, services, displays, discussion groups, practical help", as one of their leaflets describes it. There is diocesan support and a national network, and interest is growing among other denominations to follow this example. (I belong to one of these justice and peace groups where I live, although I am an Anglican, not a Catholic!) They may not be full-blown BCCs, but they have many of their characteristics and often prove to be small seeds that grow to something much larger.

What does this growth imply? Partly what David Clark suggested early on in the 1970s, that "Christians in Britain are beginning to find the centre of their spiritual life and witness in progressive, basic Christian groups (and networks) rather than in institutional structures". Twenty years on there would seem to be no diminution of that; if anything, an even greater desire to discover a "new way of being church".

"This is what we want"

The Catholic Church of the Presentation on New York's Upper Saddle River is affluent even by North American standards, perhaps an unlikely place for a small Christian community to grow — a parish where people were already "over-committed and frustrated". In 1985 the parish was celebrating 25 years, and a number of speakers had been invited to come and help reflect on those years. To facilitate discussion the congregation was divided into small groups. It had not been planned to continue these groups after that year, but "this is what we want", many said.

What was wanted was a place to make friends, to learn together about their faith and to share everyday concerns. With this brief a core group was formed to help in the formation of small Christian communities. To assist in the process, others from Brazil, Chile and the US were invited to come and share their story of forming small Christian communities (SCCs).

Soon 18 SCCs of six to fourteen people had been formed. One action these small communities undertook was to provide food and take it to soup kitchens in the

Bronx and in Newark. In all, three hundred parishioners helped with the programme. ("And what is the objective?", one of the African delegation at Notre Dame pointedly asked members who attended the consultation. "Yes, it is a programme," came the answer, "but there has to be a connection between us and the poor. We get very involved with people; it's more than just cooking and serving. For many of us this is the first time we have had any kind of relationship with poor people.")

Meeting in small groups was a new experience for those who made up these initial SCCs. Members of some groups took the Myers-Briggs personality test to help in the "getting-to-know-you" task. Regular meetings are usually divided into two parts: first prayer, scripture and life sharing, making connections between the gospel and everyday happenings, and then business and socializing. Whatever else happens grows from that.

A different example of a group that came into being in the US in the early 1980s is Communitas — a eucharist-centred community of professional people wishing to share together their faith and concerns. The community grew out of meetings of students and non-students who gathered in the 1960s at the Newman Center of George Washington University to talk together about contemporary issues. The gatherings continued throughout the 1970s, and in 1984 the decision was taken to become an autonomous community, with the name Communitas. Meetings then began to take place at a local YWCA — each Sunday a celebration of the eucharist, presided over by a priest who is either a member or a friend of the community. The homily each week takes the form of a dialogue — a "serious and mutually critical dialogue" which leads to and informs many of the social-justice commitments of the members. It is just the same kind of dialogic homily that happens each Sunday in basic Christian communities worldwide.

The majority of the 170 members live in the Washington area: students and educators, laity and religious, defence department officials and peace activists, artists, film-makers and bureaucrats, single people, couples and families with children of all ages. As a community they reflect the mobility and diversity of the greater Washington area. "In a city where vital issues and concerns confront us constantly, we feel the need to integrate more consciously our life, faith and worship," wrote Maureen Healy, a pastoral minister, and an observer at the Notre Dame consultation. [5]

Most small communities to be found throughout the US are, however, less structured than Communitas, perhaps less permanent, but no less potent. Some meet every two weeks for early breakfast at a coffee house. The author Virginia Hoffman wrote about such a community in the October 1991 issue of the British publication *The Christian*:

> When we meet we begin with each one giving thanks for something in the past week or two. We share life, in the presence of a loving God, and give each other the gift of confidentiality. Over the weeks and years we are kneading our lives together — grains of many textures — with the leaven of thanksgiving ("eucharist") and becoming one bread to share with the world. By the time we break and share our small loaf, we have already been in communion with each other and with God.

In the US a strong ecumenical movement is growing that is committed to take a public stand on issues of justice and peace. Not as well known outside America as the activities of the Religious Right (and much different from it), it has potential as a genuinely grassroots movement to help bring about change from below. "Reading the signs of the times becomes even more crucial in a period of transition — exactly where we find ourselves now," Jim

Wallis, editor of *Sojourners* monthly magazine, wrote in
spring 1993:

> On so many fronts, the old assumptions and structures that
> have long governed are dying, while the new are still
> begging to be born. The moment calls for fresh visions and
> dreams that hold the promise of change.
>
> This is especially apparent in the churches. Out of their
> institutional and spiritual crisis, a new theological conver-
> gence is occurring, with new ecumenical relationships being
> forged. The result is an emerging ground upon which
> diverse people from previously divided communities are
> finding a place to stand. Their standing and walking
> together opens up the possibility of significant and hopeful
> new configurations for the church's future and its contribu-
> tion to the wider society.

It is groups such as the ones mentioned above that are
helping to build this movement. But if the question in
Britain was "Are BCCs transferable?", the question I
encountered in the US was even more focused: Should
they be? There was a notable reticence to talk about BCCs
except in the Latin American context. It arose from a
proper concern that we Western Christians should not yet
again greedily grab on to "a piece of Latin America" in
order to profit from it ourselves, and in so doing adulterate
and tame it.

"But what next?", the parishioners of the Church of
the Presentation on Upper Saddle River asked. "But with
whom?", readers of *Sojourners* magazine pressed the
editors. Although their own vision of a new way of being
church formed and deepened month by month through the
articles they read in the magazine, many nevertheless
found it difficult to locate others of the same mind with
whom they could share the journey. Up to that point
Sojourners had been one of the groups wary of encouraging the development of American BCCs, but in spring
1993 it began its own programme to help build a faith-

based network — introducing people to each other, connecting existing groups and assisting in the formation of new small faith communities. Directing the programme initially was a Franciscan priest, Joe Nangle, who had worked with BCCs in Latin America. A new section, "Sharing the Sojourn", was added to the magazine. Included in each issue are stories of communities putting faith in action.

From Columbus, Ohio, came a story of small groups of households and individuals gathering monthly to grapple with concrete questions about consumption and simple life-styles, and to build relationships of support and challenge. Of the fifty or so persons involved, some are college students, others professionals or retirees, from several different faith backgrounds. While not exclusively faith-based, the model participants follow for their monthly reflections is the action/reflection model used by the base communities. Actions include launching a number of "learning" groups that meet to examine such topics as financial stewardship, voluntary simplicity and holistic health, and the forming of "eco-teams" — groups of five or so households that pursue a six-month course of "assessment and reduction of their own ecological consumption".[6]

A different kind of story is that of small groups of women in Appalachia who began to get together and discover one another in the 1960s. Development funds made available to these communities at that time came wholly from male-dominated institutions (including the church) through other male-dominated development organizations in Appalachia. Yet it was the women working at the grassroots who knew best the needs of the local communities. Their coming together to find and give support was not initially planned; it happened and grew into the Appalachian women's alliance, a coalition of women leaders from communities in Virginia, Tennessee,

Kentucky, West Virginia, North Carolina, Pennsylvania, Georgia and Ohio, whose aim is to improve the situation of women in the region.

In the spring of 1994 the alliance organized a caravan of women to travel through the region connecting with local women and networking with organizations addressing violence against women and community development issues.

A home for children with special needs; a small cooperative formed for marketing purposes by four Asian families; non-profit lending institutions; members of a Presbyterian congregation in Oakland, California, responding to the environmental crisis by seeking to change their own life-styles — the ways in which people come together and act together are multifarious.

Yet "SCCs are not on anyone's agenda yet", Peg Bisgrove from the Church of the Presentation told us. That was in 1991. "You know," responded Joe Healey, a Maryknoll priest who works with SCCs in East Africa, "everyone thinks that in Latin America every Catholic is a member of a basic Christian community. But take Sao Paulo as an example; only 40 percent are in BCCs. The important thing is their commitment — it colours all the rest."

Like an explosive bomb

In November 1987 some fifty participants gathered for two days in Melbourne, Australia, for a conference on basic Christian communities. Unknown to most of those attending was the upheaval that had taken place before the conference began. This was the result of a short visit by José Marins, Carolee Chanona and Teo Trevisan to Melbourne that summer. The conference organizers might never have met the Brazilian team; José, Carolee and Teo were in Melbourne on other business and the arrangement to meet was a last-minute one.

What the team shared with the Australians turned all their plans for the coming conference upside down. The encounter was later described as "like an explosive bomb". Out of the window went the prepared way of working from papers given from the platform and then responded to from the floor. Instead those who arrived found they were drawn into an experience of what basic Christian communities are all about — living, relating and working together. It became a matter of starting from people's life-situations, and from there "not only talking about things, but doing them". For those who came, the experience was so unique that participants struggled to find a word to describe the gathering — the Spanish word *convivencia* was the nearest.

One of those present had attended the intercontinental symposium in Belgium on the local church two years earlier; and from that experience he shared about the ways in which BCCs had developed in different countries. The challenge, he told participants, was to discover their own adaptation and distinctive expression of the basic Christian community. This did not, however, mean "going it alone", as Australians are wont to do. Many were aware that over the past twenty years quite a number of small communities had come into being, but most had a life-span of only eight to twelve months. In this new expression of "building community" they wanted to learn from the lessons of the past.

One of the first steps was to form a small continuing group to keep participants in touch and to help facilitate BCCs rooted in Australian soil. Volunteers were asked for, and the ecumenical nature of this new development became clear as the volunteers offered their services: they were from Anglican, Catholic, Church of Christ, Baptist and Uniting Church backgrounds.

Another early step was to produce a quarterly news-letter, *Communities Australia*. It is one of the best networking publications I know of, and from the beginning it has carried a range of articles and stories from across Australia, and also news and stories of the development of BCCs elsewhere in the world. Not "going it alone" had certainly been taken to heart. Responses from readers were positive. One from Box Hill, Victoria, wrote:

> Apart from the USA no nation in the world has such a mixture of Christian traditions in such proportions as Australia. No one denomination dominates — every street, every neighbourhood in every town and city has a whole range of Christian backgrounds in its homes. What fertile and inviting soil in which to grow vital, real praying/caring Christian community.
>
> Particularly in suburban life people need to belong, to be recognized as persons, loved and cared for.
>
> Simply put: it seems to me that the real needs of today's Australian family, the multi-denominational background of Australian people, and the unstructured, unorganized but real goodness (and faith!?) of Australians all point towards this as the new way, the Australian way of being church. [7]

Just such an expression of church is a small community meeting in an ordinary house in a busy street in Melbourne. It began with a small group of Aboriginal people who had been meeting in one another's homes to reflect on the gospel and their own deep-seated faith. In this they were helped by a religious sister. What they felt the church was saying was "Come to mass with us, be like us, we welcome you". But what they wanted was to discover how to be church in their own way. It took a while but the time came when the archdiocese leased them "a home of their own". Part of their task as a community they saw to be raising awareness of what it meant for them to discover a new way of being church.

An important step was taken in 1989 when the SCC began to use the Lumko materials from South Africa, adapting it where necessary. They began to use their own form of the "seven steps" at the time of the homily or during the eucharist. This enabled them to grow in new ways.

The central event is the Sunday eucharist, sometimes lasting two hours ("koori time"). On arrival there is time for a "cuppa and a yakka", and only when everyone has been welcomed and made comfortable will a start be made. The liturgy is informal, with opportunity for everyone to participate throughout, and afterwards there is further discussion over lunch.

Two priests asked if they could join the community, both Redemptorists, and after a period of probation they were accepted as full members (but "don't try to lead us, for we might not be able to follow"). One had come from working with BCCs in the Philippines. In this community, however, there was to be no hierarchy. Everyone has a voice. The gatherings are always informal. They do not like flashy names given to the various roles or jobs, because that is piling too many bricks on the shoulders on one person. [8]

A different story is that of the suburban parish of St Paul's Woodbridge, Logan, near Brisbane. Represented among the 10,000 people are fifty nationalities. Latin American and Filipino parishioners already had their own communities based on their own cultures, but the parish team wanted to offer this possibility to others.

The team had read widely about BCCs in other parts of the world. They began by asking parishioners at the Sunday eucharist if any would be interested in forming multi-cultural SCCs within the parish, and were surprised at the positive response. The parish structure is too big... we feel lost... we want to make friends... we need to be listened to. People began to voice their needs. Within three years the parish had six multi-cultural communities, three Filipino and one Latin American, involving over two hundred people, including children.

"The bottom line has been 'let the people speak', for if these communities are to answer the needs of Australian people, they need to grow out of our own culture," a member of the parish team has written.[9]

It is not only among Catholics that such a development is taking place. Baptist churches in the Westgate area of Melbourne were concerned over the decline of membership, and asked one of their members to write a report. While he was writing it, a new vision was born for Ross Langmead, a teacher by profession — a vision of the church discovering community and sharing it with others.

There were others who felt as he did, and an initial home meeting turned into the first of eight small "home churches", which operated alongside the more traditional Baptist churches. In time these "home churches" became the "building blocks" of a new neighbourhood church, an amalgamation of existing churches that had been on the decline. The name Westgate Baptist community was chosen to emphasize the community aspect. The one hundred or so members — a diverse group of people "who are very keen on social justice, environmental issues, feminism, new theology, local politics, third-world issues, radical discipleship" — are broken down into small groups. "A long list, but we try to accept our differences and encourage each other to pursue the Christian journey in our own way. We can't always act as a community on all of these issues."

By the time 240 people came together for a further gathering in October 1989 ("gathering" is now the preferred term) there was a sense not only of being on the way, but a "deepened sense of being in solidarity with a worldwide initiative in developing a new way of being church".[10]

In 1992 the Uniting Church of New South Wales took a big step in encouraging the development of basic Christian communities. As a response to huge population increases west of Sydney, the New South Wales synod consulted with local leaders and people at the grassroots to see how the church could grow in such a situation and help build local communities. The result was the decision to aim at developing 130 small neighbourhood congregations within ten years. These indigenous grassroots cells are called basic congregational units, and are resourced by the gifts of their members with minimal input from trained ministers.

In the same year Leonard Faulkner, the Catholic Archbishop of Adelaide, wrote about the important role of small Christian communities in the work of evangelization. His 1992 Lenten pastoral letter spoke of movements of hope, "people committed to a just and peaceful society and an ecologically sustainable approach to life". He wrote too of the central place given in the diocesan vision to "the development of small Christian communities within our parishes". "Most of us", he wrote, "need help to discover that we really matter, and that our lives are important... We need others to walk with us in small Christian communities of one kind or another, to help us discover our vocation within the context of our day-to-day lives." [11]

These developments in Australia are encouraging to the wider international network of basic Christian communities. A sense of hopeful anticipation comes through publications like *Communities Australia*. Perhaps this is due in part to the "degree of allegiance and respect" the Christian faith still commands in Australia in contrast, for instance, to Europe. Diarmuid O'Murchu writes about this in *Communities Australia* in a report on a visit made to communities there in August 1994. However, he picked up signs that this situation is changing: "... the cancer that has eaten into the church in Europe is beginning to manifest itself in Australia: deep disillusionment arising from entrenched, patriarchal power; the anger and frustration of increasing numbers of women; the disenchantment of youth, most of whom consider the church to be totally irrelevant..." He continued:

> Committed Christians face difficult decisions: "Do I hang in there and try to make it work — and for how long do I keep trying? Or do I opt for the alternatives that are beginning to spring up — the grassroots communities, the women's groups, the justice and peace movements — and commit my time and energy to birthing something that is likely to offer a more creative future?"

NOTES

[1] *Faith in the City: A Call for Action by Church and Nation*, London, Church House Publishing, 1985.

[2] *The Easter People*, report of the 1980 national pastoral congress of the Roman Catholic Church in England and Wales.

[3] John Tiller, *A Strategy for the Church's Ministry*, report presented to the general synod of the Church of England, 1983.

[4] Story written down as part of a story-telling workshop I ran in Birmingham in 1991.

[5] In *The Catholic World*, July-August 1991.

[6] *Sojourners*, January 1994.

[7] *Communities Australia*, March 1988.

[8] *Ibid.*, August 1991.

[9] *Ibid.*, November 1993.

[10] *Ibid.*, November 1990.

[11] *Hope for the Future*, pastoral letter, Lent 1992.

4. Market Place of People

> Our aim is not to form an alternative church... we want to make discoveries of the church as she was meant to be. We do this hoping for relationship and dialogue with the institutional church, so that we might share our insights on the one church as we journey.
>
> Our goal is to be where we have some possibility to change church and society.
>
> We want to change the church working from inside.

These statements, from interviews with members of BCCs in Italy, Belgium and Spain, appear in *Communities Australia*, August 1988. In a section entitled "Critical Solidarity" the writer continues:

> Critical solidarity is the term used in Europe for these relationships and the partnership between BCCs and the institutional church. It is the kind of position taken with great loyalty and integrity by the Franciscan theologian, Leonardo Boff, in Brazil. It is really the position that asks for mutual respect, the possibility of sharing experiences and insights, and also recognizing the validity of comparing our present church situation with the very different early church/biblical experience.

When talking about their aims these communities are constructive and positive, and they do not display the anti-hierarchical stance that can be too easily imputed to them.

It is perhaps because European BCCs are often viewed in this light that less is known about them — outside Europe, or indeed even within. In a recent book about base communities, *Basic Is Beautiful*, Margaret Hebblethwaite made the decision not to include them within the scope of her book for this very reason. She writes:

> I therefore have some hesitations over identifying the European groups called "base communities" as our local, inculturated version of the Latin American communities. There are many similarities — similarities, for example, in the commitment to the marginalized, in lay involvement and in liturgical creativity — but at the same time there are

differences in the way they relate to the rest of the church. Between seeing the base community as the basic cell of the church, and seeing the base community as on the fringe of, or outside, the churches, there seems to be a major theological divergence that can in no way be accounted for by cultural differences between the first world and the third world.

This is a position I have found hard to understand, and increasingly so as I have come to know a number of the communities firsthand. Since the first communities came into being in the late 1960s and early 1970s much has happened and many new steps have been taken. Grown from a number of isolated communities into national networks and from these to a European one, it is a movement that has matured, learned how to respond to change and, now thirty years on, needs to make a further radical appraisal of its position and future. The opening up of Eastern Europe and the new relationship with communities from Poland, Hungary and the Czech Republic make it all the more important to do this.

A movement church

April 1983 was the first time that members of base communities throughout Europe met together. This was at the invitation of the Christian base communities in the Netherlands, an invitation to join in their national gathering, which took place that year in Amsterdam. Representatives came from East and West Germany, Poland, Scotland, Hungary, England, Spain, Denmark, Austria, Switzerland, Portugal, France, Belgium, Italy and Nicaragua — 1500 people in all.

> I heard the heart-beat
> from the world,
> the market place of
> people,
> grassroots communities,
> Italy, Spain,

Denmark, documents,
mimeographed magazines,
charts, maps,
books, Belgium,
Amnesty International,
children and aged,
colours and numbers

Nicaragua and South Africa
peace movements
liturgy and women
the Philippines, the Germanys,
hope and song
Poland and music
Austria and seeds
hospitality
a rainbow of hope
signs for a future
mountains moving
people dancing

The type of response this coming together engendered among participants is thus captured in verse by one of the Italian participants. [1] It was an important event for all those who came, and for the development of the base movement in Europe. The differences among member countries were experienced and celebrated, and became a stretching point for many.

> There is no "official" Catholic or Protestant character to the Dutch BCC — it is a movement church. In fact, I was struck by the spirit of ecumenism there; the serenity with which they work together does not exist in Italy. I never knew who was Catholic and who was Protestant. I once again believe in the ecumenical movement.
>
> We need to be more creative and more involved with others. We are too closed within ourselves. We need a broader vision, broader contacts. We are young people who don't have the economic resources to travel, but we can do more.

It was a positive experience. I didn't expect to find so much humanity. We have a mistaken idea of these people from the North: efficiency, organization, etc. They showed a great capacity to express their feelings, they shared their lives, their houses, their bicycles. When I came, I was afraid that I would be a passive listener. Instead I was active and involved; we communicated. [2]

The success of the gathering was due to its new form and design. Some at least expected "the traditional mass meeting in the congress hall"; instead the member delegations found themselves welcomed for the first two-and-a-half days by area groupings of Dutch BCCs. They stayed in their homes, had meals together and shared experiences. The first time the entire congress met as one body was on the Saturday to share in the eucharist, to listen to an address by a Mexican Catholic bishop and to join together in a "market booth", where each member country put out literature and information about the movement in its own country and sold regional specialities for lunch.

On the final day, a Sunday, delegates were again with their host communities, joining in worship and spending time assessing the experience. One of the participants evaluated the meeting thus: "It is very useful to have this type of encounter, because beyond seeing the extension of the movement and the number of people who think like we do, we now know that there is in Europe and in the world — we touched it directly here — a great grassroots movement, ecumenical in the real sense of the word, which is taking root and growing."

A decision taken by the end of the meeting was to repeat the experience in two years. This time it was the Italians' turn to be host, and they invited representatives from other member delegations to join them in planning the event.

Simple, plain and austere

This second gathering of the European BCCs took place in Turin in April 1985. In fact this too was a national gathering to which representatives from other countries were invited. However, planning for the congress was a shared task, and a preparatory report was compiled to which twelve countries contributed. This was the first attempt to draw together a synthesis of what was held in common by all the communities.

The picture that emerges is of communities largely made up of middle-class people, but predominantly living in working-class areas, on the outskirts of cities where the problems of unemployment, drug addiction, delinquency and isolation are most severe. Most members are politically left-wing, but in a broad rather than in a partisan or militant sense. A large number have chosen to be members of various grassroots movements for change. (While it is true that the majority of members are middle-class, present in many of the communities are people from lower middle-class backgrounds and more marginalized groups. Few are from upper-class backgrounds.)

The communities hold in common the aim of building a church "in solidarity with the poor", and work for this in practical ways such as, for example, following a simple, plain and even austere life-style, and in many cases adopting the normal life-style of the poor in the areas where they live. There is a sharing of goods within the communities themselves, and a practical working out of human and financial solidarity with those in need at the local level and with people in the third world. In all, what strikes one is the commitment to and active participation in the struggles of the poor and working for the autonomy of the church at the grassroots level.

The close relation between faith and socio-political involvement is considered essential — the incarnation of faith in daily life as a requirement which comes from the mission of Christ in the world and as a way of sharing love for one's neighbour. It is this faith that undergirds the individual's attitudes, and gives strength for the struggles that arise and ultimate meaning to them. On a communal level it is this faith that leads to analysis and action, most often arising from biblical reflection.[3]

Turin was the first European congress I attended. This was before I had visited any of the communities, and I was surprised to find it so middle-class. I was actually rather comforted by this fact, as I felt here was a movement with which I could identify as one who shared their background. Members of the communities had their own comments to make on this issue of middle- or working-class orientation, seeing it as part of the process that is needed in Europe — the liberation of the middle classes which can only come about through their encounter with the marginalized, the oppressed and the exploited. Many commented on the general atmosphere of disillusionment, frustration and lack of enthusiasm in several European countries with political and "democratic" institutions.

Rights of indigenous peoples

The first all-European congress took place in Bilbao, in the Basque region of Spain, in 1987.

The first BCCs appeared in the Basque region in the mid to late 1970s. In Vitoria this came about in 1976 as the result of a strike by factory workers. Since such action was at that time illegal, a church was used as a meeting place. The police threw smoke bombs into the church, and when those inside came out they were fired upon; five were killed. Church people were so angered by this that they met together to decide what their response should be. The local bishop did not approve of this, although others in the hierarchy were sympathetic, and there were priests who, in the beginning, acted as coordinators. The questions raised by the strikers and the response of those in authority opened up others. These lay men and women were asking themselves in each case what a Christian response should be, and what action should be taken. Their analysis of the situation raised further questions. One member commented: "It was seen to be important to face up to the ideology of the church — which was in fact oppressive to poor people instead of seeking their liberation."[4]

The communities which came into being in the mid to late 1970s began to coordinate their activities in the early 1980s. From that time they took the name Christian popular communities, all three words pointing to essential components of the CPC. The *popular* element came about as a result of a number of steps (as in the Philippines); it was a big step to change from social service to a more involved struggle, from assistance to a commitment with society. It was a journey that has led the communities to the place where commitment to society becomes real "in the struggle for freedom and for individuals and collective rights as a nation", as a report on CPCs of Basque country, written in preparation for the European seminar, says. It puts the CPCs in the forefront of the struggles of the Basque peoples for self-determination, with the particular aim of helping to bring it about through dialogue between the Spanish government and the Basque people. Their active participation in this issue of self-determination gives rise to reflection that goes well beyond the Basque question and the Basque region. Given what has happened in Eastern Europe since the fall of the Berlin wall, the report concludes that "controlled democracy is not participative... We think it becomes unavoidable that the economic, social and political pattern should be built by each people freely, with its imagination, creativity and participation."

Since this meeting was being held in Bilbao, representatives from other countries prepared by reading papers and by seeking to understand at greater depth the situation of the Basque peoples. There was no common response; there were questions, and further questions surfaced in the course of the congress. Many went away with a new appreciation of the struggles of the Basque peoples, and the need to understand, and to identify more closely with, all those worldwide seeking their collective rights. Later, at the fourth congress held in Paris in 1991, there was to be a moving encounter between those from the Basque country and representatives from Wales attending a congress for the first time. One of the Welsh representatives was a member of the Welsh nationalist movement, several times imprisoned for civil disobedience activities. He went with the Basque representatives to join in a protest action on behalf of political prisoners held in a Parisian gaol; he and his Basque friends could not understand each other's language, but "there at the prison gates we didn't need language; it was the same cause, the same sense of why we were there as Christians". Others at Bilbao had different experiences, but most of them would have agreed with what one said later, that it was "an opening of my eyes to the very limited and partial outlook which each of us can cultivate".[5]

There were tensions that had not been apparent at the earlier gatherings; questions that were to be faced and discussed at greater length within the collective at future meetings. There were, however, other sides to the congress. "Relaxed, spontaneous and very noisy!" was the appreciative comment of a representative from Scotland. It had started that way with a shared meal; and the next day tired weekend travellers recovered further when they were taken to the countryside outside Bilbao to be welcomed, wined and dined by members of BCCs. As usual, it was a struggle to be understood and to understand, and yet "a few words and lots of gestures went a long way", as my Scottish friend wrote later. Language limitations were undoubtedly a contributory factor in the tensions that had arisen at Bilbao. The problems were never serious, and representatives left with "see you in two years time". European congresses had now become a part of the life of European BCCs.

Peaceful means of struggle

Squatters in a camp in the middle of Paris, on the site of the new much-publicized national library, welcomed a small group from the fourth congress of basic Christian communities. The squatters were African workers and refugees, victims of discrimination, forced into a tented ghetto through lack of housing. It was an important visit for those who made it, bringing home yet once again the importance of the congress theme: "Social Justice in the Europe of 1992: A Challenge for Basis Christian Communities".

The preparation for this congress included an in-depth analysis of the effects of the open market on those at the base of society, and also on third-world countries. How far the rights of the poorest and most marginalized were safeguarded was a key criterion to determine the soundness or otherwise of social and economic policies. One keynote speaker summed this up with a challenging question: "Doesn't the urgency of the times consist in bringing the social question up to date as a peaceful means of struggle in a world where ethics, as well as human rights, are in worldwide peril?"[6]

Ulrich Duchrow spoke of the role of BCCs in a more global context. He considered first the ambiguous situation in which many church leaders found themselves when confronted with issues of social justice, largely because of the way in which most clerical institutions had become dependent on financial institutions and the way they work. Even more dangerous was the stance of fundamentalist groups and movements that adapt themselves to capitalism without question and preach an individualistic doctrine of salvation that prevents their adherents from making any serious social and political commitment.

In strong contrast he addressed the BCCs present:

> Be glad in the first place that you *are*! You are yourselves a sign of God's loving creative power, of the power of God's spirit to transform people from self-centred individuals into a people of a new community with God and with each other. There are, of course, conflicts and crises in BCCs also, but you are the proof that such things can be solved in another way than by oppression and violence. So you are the salt of the earth and the light of the world. It is exactly because of the many disappointments with the institutional churches that you are, for many Christians, a source of hope.

But after the revolution...

For the first time, in Paris there was adequate representation from basic Christian communities in Eastern Europe. Some contact had been made with these communities before the collapse of the iron curtain in 1989, but for the most part it had not been possible for those in Eastern European countries to attend such gatherings. With little contact possible, it was difficult to know how similar or dissimilar the communities were, or how much they had in common.

In the group I was part of at the Paris congress there were members from the Czech Republic, and today there is ongoing representation from there on the European collective. One community had its beginning in 1974 when a group of young Catholics, 15-25 years old, began to meet unofficially to study theology, at first once a fortnight, then more often. They had the encouragement and support of academics. A further step was taken in 1977 when one of the group was ordained to the diaconate, and others were entrusted with the roles of readers and acolytes.

Another key moment in the life of the community came with their developing an "authentic liturgical life, which in a natural way grows from the mundane needs of everybody". In this too they saw the importance of "the function of the presbyter growing 'in a natural way' from the community and not imposed from the outside".

The community began also to meet together annually for a full week, changing the venue each time. They had to do this because the secret police had become interested in them. They had also to follow basic security precautions — no information given over the telephone, singing only when they were sure they could not be heard, taking care not to park cars in front of the building in which they were meeting. It was with difficulty that the little group survived, but by 1988 it had grown so large that it had to divide into two groups, with lots cast to decide one's membership!

With the fall of the communist regime, the community had to make more difficult decisions. Should the group be dissolved? Should they all become members of more traditional churches? Such questions are still asked, but the community continues, and remains open mainly for "people on the fringes of the church, who find it difficult to find their place in the official structures."

"But after the revolution..." Or was it "before the revolution"? It is all so close, so present, and hearing these words I am immediately drawn again into the events of 1989. "Since the revolution..." A friend from Hungary talks of the many young people who have been drawn to the communities. Amidst all the complexities that freedom has brought, perhaps, they think, here is a clear direction. And yet, my friend tells us, many of the communities themselves are now becoming less critical, more quiescent. Nothing is predictable.

A new resistance movement

Now, in 1995, it is not only communities in the former Eastern European countries that are struggling to stay on course. Age and exhaustion are beginning to tell on the effectiveness of many of the BCCs in Western Europe as well.

In a report written in preparation for the next gathering of European communities to take place in late 1995, Swiss BCCs say that many groups are "tired out", that some of the early communities have disappeared, and that the politically active groups seem to be most in trouble. New communities that have arisen do not last for long. "At the moment Christian base communities are not growing bigger: they are growing more grey-haired" — the Dutch BCCs echo much the same feeling of decline as the Swiss. This crisis in some of the communities has led the European collective to opt for a smaller gathering this time where more in-depth sharing can take place among representatives.

Yet while a midlife-type crisis is evident in communities in a number of countries and regions, in other places there is the feeling that growth has only just started. This is true in England, Ireland, Scotland and Wales; Austria has newly joined the collective; and those from Eastern European countries rejoice that they are now given a new opportunity for growth. French-speaking Belgium has recently established a coordinating team. All of this brings an interesting dynamic to the collective. [6]

Against this background there are also other new developments. Women's groups continue to be strong, and their number is rising. The collective has a close relationship to Kairos Europa. Part of a worldwide movement that started in South Africa in 1985, Kairos Europa works for justice within Europe. It traces its beginnings to the meeting on justice, peace and the integrity of creation at 1989 in Basel and the people's parliament that met in

1992 in Strasbourg. Similar themes concerning the emerging European Union were being pursued, and the two networks have much in common. Kairos Europa's new programme "Spirituality of Resistance in Europe" continues the call to a resistance which includes "hope and liberation" and is a consequence of metanoia, a conversion, which enables each to enter into the struggles and conflicts of others. It too recognizes the important place of communities that enable such a conversion to take place.

It is likely that many more such "liberation movements" will be born in the coming decade; a new wave, born of the turn of the century. If they complement each other and work together, there is hope indeed that a real grassroots revolution may be under way.

"It is important that we become visible," one member from Belgium said at a recent gathering. It is for this reason that the European base communities have since the 1960s come together in networks — regional, national and European. Now as other similar networks come into existence, there is at least the possibility that an effective resistance movement will emerge.

At the end of his address to the 1991 European congress in Paris, Ed de la Torre asked all of us to close our eyes. "... so you can see the darkness," he said. "Do not be afraid to see, to acknowledge that the darkness has become even darker... But also look at the many torches in the darkness, in so many different places in the world — some few and flickering, others quite bright... Wherever you can imagine darkness, you can also imagine light..."

He then asked us to clap. To clap first with one finger, then two, then three, then four, then all. The sound built up to a crescendo. It was like rain falling, gently, then a deluge. "We need," Ed told us, "to have ears to listen, even as we struggle. We might feel like clapping with one finger, but if we hear the many others, we feel less lonely and weak. We need to look at our other fingers; maybe we are using only one, or two."

There are, he concluded, still resources and energies waiting to be discovered and mobilized for justice.

NOTES

[1] Poem initialled ejg in *The Bridge*, Italian ecumenical news agency, June-July 1983 newsletter.

[2] Responses to the gathering from Italian BCC members, in *ibid*.

[3] Preparatory report for second European congress of basic Christian communities, Turin, 1985.

[4] Interview by Ian Fraser, 1983, included in *Wind and Fire*, Scottish Churches House, 1986.

[5] Louise Dunphy, personal report on the Congress.

[6] This section is compiled from reports written in preparation for the European seminar to take place at the end 1995.

5. How Can Dialogue Take Place?

"The Bible is a faithful companion in the struggle, always present, as the water of the river which carries the little boat of the CEBs."[1]

The 1980s were a period of continued consolidation and growth for the BCCs in Latin America, although increasingly accompanied in many parts by severe persecution leading sometimes even to martyrdom. Such circumstances were for the moment to aid rather than hinder the growth of the communities. The gospel message which they lived and proclaimed exposed injustices and brutality. And biblical reflection was at the very heart of this confrontation.

Carried by the river

In July 1985 the first Latin American pastoral biblical consultation was held in Bogota, Colombia. Bishops, scripture teachers and pastoral-biblical experts came together with priests, religious and laity, both women and men, from 22 countries. Twenty years had passed since the Second Vatican Council had "expressed with all clarity, as had never been done before, that we and our fellow bishops throughout the world have the serious responsibility to do everything within our power to see to it that the people have easy access to sacred scripture".[2]

Latin American bishops had indeed taken this responsibility seriously; Medellín and Puebla had clearly shown this to be so. Through these two events, "the church profoundly renewed its evangelizing strength, insisting upon the reading of the Bible at all levels in the church and in every social strata, especially among the poor".[3]

Indeed, the poor "are reading the Bible on a massive scale". They "are doing this in the Sunday liturgy, in the basic ecclesial communities, in fraternal meetings, in Christian assemblies..., in family catechesis and in many apostolic movements which are developing within the people of God".

In the mountains of Guatemala an ecumenical group of villagers met to consider the passage from Luke 4 where Jesus reads the ancient scripture that speaks of "good news to the poor". "Jesus wasn't only talking about the rights of the poor in the next life. It's clear that he was concerned with the sorrows of people in this world as well," they concluded.

What did this mean for them? Two-thirds of the land in Guatemala is owned by a few rich Guatemalans; others, like the native Indians living in this village, eke out an existence as best they can. Many die from illnesses related to malnutrition. Poor themselves, the members of this small ecumenical group decided to put the good news into practice, to help those even poorer. They dug a fishpond and filled it with fish from a nearby lake; they bought a small plot of land and planted garlic — the fish for better nutrition, the garlic to sell in order to provide a fund for the sick and for emergencies.

Their work is carried out against a background of constant fear of attack by the Guatemalan army. Any who take such action, however small, are considered a threat and a likely target; in a neighbouring village three hundred men, women and children had been slaughtered by soldiers in 1982. [4]

For villagers like these many of the gospel stories are close indeed to their daily experience. It does not surprise them to read that Jesus, having proclaimed the good news to the poor, was dragged out of town by an angry mob intent on taking his life.

Often in Latin America the Bible has been the means of changing the lives of entire communities. In the north of Ecuador two neighbouring indigenous tribes feuded for many years. Drunkenness most often fuelled the violence. Then small Bible reflection groups began to arise, animated by indigenous catechists. Those reading the Bible faced the need to do something about the mutual hostility that existed. There was stubborn resistance within the communities. Then one day a eucharist was celebrated to which members of both groups came. Before the mass, scripture texts were read and reflected on. Then came the moment when the miracle happened and the two communities embraced each other — a transformation that has been sustained.[5]

A new kind of ecumenism

That Catholics should be outdoing Protestants in reading the Bible and forming Bible circles was a new phenomenon in Latin America, as indeed elsewhere in the world. But although the base community movement in Latin America has developed largely among Roman Catholics, it is not wholly so.

Dave and Tina Cave from the Anfield Road Fellowship in Liverpool, England, talked to Baptists, Lutherans and Moravians when they visited BCCs in Central America in 1988. Dave is a Baptist minister, and he and Tina visited a Baptist church in San Salvador whose members did not want to be named or photographed. This church had been "born out of social concern and the way the Bible confronted the people with the fact that Jesus came to serve, not to be served". The New Testament book of James, with its passion for social justice, had become a focus for reflection and action.

The cost of this concern, Dave and Tina discovered, had been persecution, death, exile and disappearances. Forty families from the church had been exiled, five people had disappeared and two had been assassinated. Several said their commitment had been deepened as a result of the others' witness.[6]

In Nicaragua they met the principal of Managua Baptist seminary, Roque Savalla, who told them of a change that had taken place among Baptists in the 1960s and 1970s. The Somoza government's oppressive regime had caused many to question what was happening and to ask themselves what their response should be. Managua seminary had become a place where regular biblical reflection took place. Conservatism and a rigid fundamentalism had largely given place to openness and concern. Numerous Baptists became involved in the Sandinista revolution, as couriers or in hiding fugitives. This openness, and the desire to be involved in matters of peace and social justice, had continued beyond the overthrow of the Somoza government.

In December 1972 a major earthquake in Managua killed 20,000 people and destroyed 600 blocks of buildings — hotels, restaurants and department stores. Five days later, a group of Protestant leaders formed a relief committee to provide food, medical help, temporary housing and burials. Supplying these needs brought them face to face with the unjust system of distribution that existed in the city, and they decided that more than emergency relief was needed. In this way CEPAD (Evangelical Committee for Aid to Development) came into being to put the work they had begun on a permanent basis. Its work now embraces development in areas of agriculture, housing, health and community work, human rights, church relations, women's work, youth work, and theology and education.

Particularly in the countries that had been or were ruled by oppressive regimes, such as Nicaragua, El Salvador, Guatemala and Honduras, Protestants were most challenged about the social aspects of the gospel, as the Caves were told. Not all were prepared to be challenged in this way; there were those who still affirmed a "Protestant heritage of non-involvement". Where BCCs were emerging among Protestants, the use of the Bible was always a primary element in their formation, alongside the search for cultural identity and dealing with problems of marginalization.

That BCCs can and do arise out of any denomination or none makes for a new kind of ecumenism — "functional rather than institutional," one parish priest said to the Caves. A WCC team visiting Brazil in 1988 came across a young community that was growing up in a town on the outskirts of Brasilia. It was animated by a young woman priest from the USA. A sense of community was developing, decisions were being taken together, plans were being shared to build a house as a women's centre. "The fact that this was an Episcopal church made no difference to the people. Those who lived locally, of whatever background, saw it as their church, and in any case, we were told, there is potential for a church on every street!"[7]

An Episcopalian minister, Orlando Guerrero, whom I met in England in 1992, told me about another development. A Venezuelan, he had encouraged the formation of BCCs in his parish, having seen what was happening in nearby Catholic parishes. During the formative stages, he had stayed closely in touch with his Catholic friends, continuing to draw help and inspiration from them. What had impressed him most was "a different kind of ministry, where you stand back and let others take up their responsibility; encourage rather than dominate". Orlando's story and others seem to indicate that perhaps there are many more Protestant BCCs in Latin America and other predominantly Catholic countries than we yet know of.

In search of the promised land

A swaying, dancing crowd of 1600 people from twenty Latin American countries heralded the beginning of the sixth inter-ecclesial meeting of the Brazilian basic Christian communities in Trinidade, Goiania, in the summer of 1986. There were Lutherans, Presbyterians, Methodists and Episcopalians here too, although only one Baptist.

The theme of the week was "Basic Christian Communities: People of God in Search of the Promised Land". Still searching, even though military rule had ended some five years previously. Many present feared that little had changed, that the new republic was in essence only the same old reality under a different name. The changes that had taken place were in the popular movements themselves, and in the churches. The movement for agrarian reform, which had been armed in the 1960s, now organized itself for non-violent action. The church that had once colluded with those in power now stood arm-in-arm with the disempowered. Its programme of awareness-building had changed the consciousness of the mass of people.

A month before the assembly, some two hundred landless workers had marched to the state capital, Porto Alegre, where some took over the parliament building, while others camped in front of the land reform headquarters. They were demanding 32,000 hectares of land which had been promised to them but still not given. Their demands were supported by a statement signed by 54 bishops. Fifty percent of their demands were met. Wrote Derek Winter, the only Baptist attending the assembly, in a report on the meeting:

> Much of the credit for this kind of movement must undoubtedly go to the work of the basic Christian communities. There must be some 100,000 of these scattered all over Brazil, from the remotest areas of Para and Rondonia to the huge and terrifying sprawl of Sao Paulo. Representing perhaps no more than 5 percent of the population, they have had an impact on the national life out of all proportion to their numbers. This has happened through the movements they have spawned — for human rights, for direct elections, for political amnesty, for better living conditions. The movement is still gathering momentum.

The 1980s had been potent years for the BECs throughout Latin America, small communities growing in strength and maturity. Towards the end of the decade a pastoral message was sent to the Mexican base ecclesial communities by twelve Mexican bishops and three archbishops. In it they re-committed themselves to "promote, orient and accompany" the BECs, and said simply that they wanted "to share the fate of the poor by accompanying them as pastors in their struggles and hopes".

They encouraged the BECs to continue along the same path: "Cooperate in the emergence of a new society, maintaining your evangelical presence in genuine and popular movements, and contributing to the consolidation of those efforts that seek justice and liberation. As the church that you are, put yourself at the service of the poorest." Then they went further:

> The BECs, being church at the base, also present a challenge and a perspective for the church as a whole. For this reason we call upon all the people of God whom we serve to recognize the Spirit that enlivens and strengthens the BECs. Through incarnating among the poor, they show the way of the gospel in this history. The communitarian experience of the church is rejuvenated within the BECs through the participation of the lay people and the new configurations of the traditional ministries. The BECs have been able to make the gospel a good news for the poor and, at the same time, a denunciation of the sin in the world.

There were however difficult problems to face as the communities entered the 1990s. A greater measure of support would be needed — and it was forthcoming.

What kind of conversation?

> This is a moment I have dreamed about, but I did not think it would come so soon. The moment when there would be a worldwide coming together of those in small Christian

communities. I knew it needed to happen and would happen, but I did not think that I would live to see it.

Christopher Mwoleka from Tanzania was sharing his happiness with those of us gathered at Maryknoll seminary in New York for a week's orientation programme prior to the consultation at Notre Dame. Hearing him say that, and later hearing his story and that of the other Africans present, brought tears to my eyes, as sharing it had to his. A member of a small Christian community in a rural parish, Christopher Mwoleka also happens to be the diocesan bishop, but it is first as a member of an SCC that he introduces himself.

At Maryknoll we were Africans, Europeans and North Americans; at Notre Dame we would also be with those from Latin America and from Asia. One reason the conference was held at all was the fact that the BECs in Latin America were facing serious problems. Their witness was on the one side undermined by the action of the Vatican, and on the other weakened by many of their members joining sects and Pentecostal groups. "It is a tired moment in Latin America," one of the Brazilian delegates was to tell us at Notre Dame. This coming together with representatives from communities all around the world was one way to give encouragement, to demonstrate that the base community movement had extended beyond Latin America, and to facilitate ongoing networking.

It was at several points a painful encounter. Of the representatives only two of us were Protestants. That caused at times consternation and embarrassment. It also highlighted the fact that while it was international, the conference was hardly ecumenical.

Not, I think, that it was meant to be, and the two of us were glad enough to be there. I was also aware that we Protestants have much to thank the Catholic Church for in pioneering this "new way of being church", and was glad to say so publicly.

There were also the only too obvious differences in life-style. To visit the affluent Church of the Presentation in Upper Saddle River with our new friends from small Christian communities in Tanzania, Kenya and Sierra Leone, to be with them in the homes of members of one of Presentation's small Christian communities, was to wonder how there could be any connection between the two experiences. "But I have heard today of people who are lonely, divorced, bereaved, with few to support or comfort them. Such sadness here too, and with less support than in an African village or town," Christopher Mwoleka said, providing another perspective.

At the end of the consultation a letter was drafted which dealt with its background and concluded with reflections and recommendations. It was a letter addressed to "members of small Christian communities, to leaders of our churches, and to all those concerned about the future of our churches". Part of it reads:

> Basic Christian communities are a phenomenon in Christian churches throughout the world. While Vatican II may not have foreseen a worldwide small community movement, the two are causally connected... Small Christian communities... have never been internationally orchestrated; they just began happening everywhere, with many basic similarities. Small Christian communities see the Spirit of God at work empowering Christians through membership in this rather sudden phenomenon.
>
> One of the recommendations from the meeting was to create a greater ecumenical climate for ongoing dialogue; another was to encourage interfaith dialogue.

There are other ways of coming together.

"Tell me about your dream? What do you hope will happen here?" I asked the young Baptist minister, one month into his first full-time appointment, an appointment shared with his wife and with another couple.

Tim Presswood's answer was revealing. He told me of their reluctance to impose any agenda, because "if we are going to take seriously the idea of a church that is listening to the local community, then that listening process has to be real".

He continued:

> That is not to say that we don't have an agenda. I personally would be very happy to do away with the church building altogether, and to think of the church as being a network of small... call them house groups, call them cell groups... But at this stage it would be wholly inappropriate to share that dream with the church community because one of the very key things is that we want to minister with the members of this church, and primarily to be enablers. After all, they are the people who have lived here all their lives.

Tim and Deborah Presswood and Tim and Caroline Clay share an unusual appointment, and this is partly the result of a number of factors. One is the fact that at present in the UK there are just too many Baptist ministers for the number of assignments available; another is that the smaller, poorer Baptist churches are the ones most likely to be without a minister, being unable to pay one. Mersey Street Baptist tabernacle in Manchester's Openshaw falls into this category.

Yet another factor is the personal journeys of the Presswoods and Clays, and in particular the impact made on them by spending three weeks in El Salvador and encountering basic ecclesial communities there. Three weeks which they continue to live and relive — "I can go on for ever about El Salvador," Tim said, as I was about to bring the interview with him to a close.

The visit to El Salvador took place in the early 1990s. A group of five went from Northern Baptist College in

Manchester, their itinerary arranged through David Mee, a Baptist minister in El Salvador. They were under no illusion about the risks involved; there was a war on at the time. Most of their time was spent with the basic ecclesial community whose story is told in Pablo Galdamez' *Faith of a People*. Not quite the community that existed in the period 1970-80, but one of several that had grown out of that original community.

I wanted to know what they had learned:

> Immediately you are thrown into something of what being a community is all about, which is solidarity, support..., comfort. Even in those circumstances, making a safe space for one another.
>
> Then hope. That hope was very real and very tangible; it was evident in the faces of the people we met, and it showed itself in the work they were doing. These people knew what they wanted and they were working to get it — peace with justice. In a place like Openshaw, with second- and third-generation unemployed people who have been told that they are dirty scroungers and believe it, hope is important. Now I know that's rather simplistic, because in El Salvador since the peace accords that hope has been severely jeopardized; nevertheless...

Hope *is* needed in Openshaw. Mersey Street Baptist tabernacle does not exactly have a thriving congregation — numerically. Or much future, unless something changes. The seventeen or so members are made up of "fifteen little old ladies and two men". Two are under sixty, all the others over seventy. What they do have going for them is the fact that they have lived all their lives in that neighbourhood and experienced the changes that have taken place (mostly for the worse), and have a dogged commitment to their church and to the local community.

"They would make a super basic Christian community were it not for the fact they are all so old." This was a chance remark of a tutor at Northern Baptist College, but one that caught Tim Presswood's imagination. And on his return from El Salvador he was sent on placement to Mersey Street Baptist tabernacle. A little later, the Clays and the Presswoods raised the question tentatively with the principal of Northern Baptist College, Brian Haymes: "What if the four of us went together to Openshaw with the idea of putting the principles of basic Christian communities into practice?" The principal was interested and willing to take this further; the institutional wheels were set in motion, and the Openshaw project received formal blessing. There was no money, however, to fund it. The two couples would have to be self-supporting. The two women have full-time jobs — Deborah is a teacher, Carolyn a food consultant. In 1994 Tim Clay was working part-time in a hospice, and Tim Presswood partly as a house husband, minding two-year-old Rachel while working to refurbish the nearly derelict house he and Deborah were buying. It worked fine, he said, "as long as folk realize that if I go to call on them or go to a meeting in the daytime Rachel and her toys come too". The Clays lived nearby. Sadly Tim Clay was killed in a climbing accident in the summer of 1994. The project, nevertheless, continues to work towards building "a network of small... call them house groups, call them cell groups..." Tim Presswood had stumbled in trying to find the right words. What is built will be whatever emerges and is appropriate to Openshaw. El Salvador was an important part of the journey, but is not the model.

A similar story comes from North America. Bruce Henning is a pastor working among the urban poor. He has regularly visited base communities in Latin America and been influenced by them in his life and work. He writes that there is "a conversion that comes from non-tourist travel to third-world countries. It challenges one's theology, ecclesiology, politics, economics and life-style..."

The travel is not one-way only. Many priests and sisters have returned to their native lands to share with the local church the experience and possibilities of basic Christian communities. In England Fr Ed O'Connell came from working with basic Christian communities in Peru to share his experience with small justice and peace groups throughout England. In the USA I met a priest who had returned from Guatemala to do much the same. We were both visiting a small Christian community in Connecticut. I was there for the afternoon, but he expected to stay for some time in Connecticut helping to facilitate SCCs in that area.

How can this kind of sharing become more mutual? Karin Granberg-Michaelson raises this question in her book *Healing Community*:

> The North in fact is arrogant and cannot imagine what it needs to learn from the experience of the poor in traditional cultures of the South. Yet it is in the cries of the people for liberation from all forms of injustice that we are all awakened to the vision of the reign of God and the need for the church to respond in a peaceful revolution so that righteousness and peace at last will join hands.
>
> ... These communities of liberation are sounding a call to the rest of the church to respond to the cries of all people. But what does the South have to teach the North about creating healing communities? And how can this dialogue take place?[8]

Scholar and activist Ched Myers focuses even more acutely on this question:

> A small but growing number of first-world Christians have come to see liberation theologians as our primary dialogue partners. But what kind of conversation are we having with them? Our partners are rightly concerned at the way their work can (and has) so easily and subtly become a novel (and even exotic) commodity in first-world ecclesial and theological market-places... Theologies of liberation claim to be

reflection on practice and mere commentary on someone else's practice deftly sidesteps our own. Even if we sympathize with theologies of liberation, we are in constant danger of expropriating their rhetoric without engaging their methods. A midweek Bible study group in our local parish does not become a "base community" just because it is so renamed, nor are we in solidarity with the poor simply by declaring we are. This is why liberation theologians have become more insistent that we who claim to understand and concur with their basic assertions must discern our own context, respond with our own practice, and reflect critically on that.[9]

Lord, forgive us

I had taken with me to the Notre Dame consultation Christian Aid's *Living the Good News*, the 1992 Lenten book which contained stories of basic Christian communities in Brazil, Guatemala, Haiti and El Salvador. I held the book up for all to see during our European presentation to the consultation, and explained that in the coming Lent Christians throughout Britain and Ireland would be meeting in small groups to read week by week these stories and to consider the questions posed by them. The book well fitted our overall presentation as we had started it by involving the whole conference in an acted history lesson of the colonization of Latin America by Europeans. The publication of *Living the Good News* had been planned to coincide with the commemoration of Christopher Columbus's arrival in the Caribbean. The introduction spoke of the priests who had journeyed with the first colonizers, bringing the good news of the gospel. "Yet along with the good news went much that was bad news for the people of that region. Europeans did not only baptize the people, they also made slaves of them, stripping them of their wealth and destroying their cultures."

"Bravo! Bravo!" The Latin Americans came afterwards to thank us for being in solidarity with them. With the language barrier, what was lacking in words was conveyed well enough through looks and hugs. The next morning at breakfast one of the Brazilian team came to ask if they could have the book to take home with them to show others. "It makes a difference to us to know this is happening," they said. I gladly gave the booklet, but asked in return to take a photograph of the five of them, with one of them holding up the booklet. This story had another delightful sequel. I was at a small meeting in London and those of us attending had been asked to take along some small symbol of "new ways of being church"; I had taken this photograph. I told its story, and afterwards discovered that one of those present had helped in the writing of the book by gathering the material. She in turn wanted a copy of the photograph — to take back to share with others at Christian Aid office. "Connections like this encourage us to keep going."

That Lent I was part of a small group that met in my home to study *Living the Good News*. Throughout the parish other groups were meeting. The stories, the Bible passages, the prayers, all helped us reflect on one issue the group had chosen to work on together over the six weeks — the issue of homelessness. However, it proved a difficult exercise for us as a group to reflect on together, and to agree at the end on any action to take. We did become enmeshed, I believe, in the kind of superficiality that Ched Myers warns against. If our group had remained together for more than those six weeks, perhaps it would have been different.

In contrast is a study on marginalization undertaken by Anfield Road Fellowship for the European congress of basic Christian communities in 1991. The Fellowship is a "a sort of base community cum house church" in a poor neighbourhood of Liverpool. You can only be a member if you live within walking distance of Anfield Road. Their case study was called "Marginalization — a View from the Underside". Here were people who knew well what it feels like to be marginalized:

☆ Angry	☆ Upset
☆ Frustrated	☆ Isolated
☆ Inferior	☆ Upset
☆ You get bitter	☆ You try to forget it
☆ You lose confidence	☆ You go into yourself
☆ You stay away from people and situations that put you down	☆ You put their windows in
☆ You hide what you have or haven't got	☆ You don't let your weaknesses show
☆ You get depressed	☆ You feel rejected
☆ You become an inverted snob	☆ You feel sorry for them
☆ There's nothing you can do	☆ You can mix and challenge
☆ It makes you determined	

They drew diagrams:

"Pushed aside"   "Left out"   "Looked-down on"

They considered different case studies. One went as follows:

People have gathered for a Bible study you are taking on the letter of James in the New Testament. One talks about a new car they have just bought. Someone else has just had their house taken over by the bailiffs because they couldn't afford the poll tax. The two people get into a very heated argument. You are in charge of the meeting. How do you handle things?

A very lively discussion followed! They thought about what the Bible had to say about "all this". The starting point was: "What could we think of or remember?"

"The first shall be last and the last first" (we didn't know where that came from but A. will investigate).

Jesus chose Peter but Peter felt too sinful. "Get away. I am very sinful."

The disciples asked Jesus who was the greatest.

I will never leave you or forsake you. "He is there for you."

Who were the outcasts in Jesus' day? Lepers, Samaritans, tax collectors, gentiles.

We looked at the disciples arguing about who was the greatest and Jesus putting a child in the middle of the circle and say, "The least of you is the greatest."

"It is no big shame to be at the bottom, Jesus stands there with us."

"Jesus turns it inside out and on its head."

"If people want to put God at the centre or at the top he says the poor are there with him. If they put some people at the bottom or outside, he says he is there with them."

This way of reading the Bible is a lot closer to the way it is read in BCCs in the South. Part of our difficulty in Britain and other northern countries is that we are largely oriented as Christians to a different way of reading the Bible. I learned over the years to take the biblical text more or less as it was on the page, and to reflect on it as it spoke to my own personal life and my need at that time. Bible or sharing groups that I have been part of have had a similar orientation.

To read the Bible in its own context, to let it challenge and confront the society of which I am part and for that to be a communal experience is still new to me, as to many others I know. I can still feel the shock that went through me as a result of studying the parable of the talents this way. I had my own interpretation of this parable that I often shared with others. It was that if I perceived God to be as ruthless and uncaring as the king is in this parable, then I would bury my talents (gifts) in the ground, and not grow as a result.

I did find it difficult to equate God with the kind of king portrayed, but I had found a way round this and I still saw the parable as having to do only with my own personal walk with God. When, together with others, I looked at the parable in its own context I began to see that it was more likely that Jesus was not saying that God was like this king, but rather the opposite, and that he had told the story to warn his disciples about such exploitation and to say to them that there are no quick fixes either.

Chatting one evening in The Hague with Gea Boessen-kool and Jan-Willem, in whose home I stayed when visiting Ekklesia, we talked about different approaches to studying the Bible. "In the Lord's prayer we say 'forgive us our debts, as we forgive our debtors...' Now what do those debts mean? Do we think it applies, for example, to the debts of third-world countries? I think it applies to that too," said Jan-Willem.

Purifying the air we breathe
This matter of forgiveness was on the table at Santo Domingo, the most recent gathering of the Latin American bishops. October 1992 coincided with the quincentenary of Columbus's arrival in the Americas, and it was seen as an occasion for taking stock of the church's role in the Americas in those five hundred years. The Brazilian bishops present proposed that at the end of the conference a penitential liturgy be held when the church would ask

pardon "for the abuses of the past", especially for the suffering inflicted on the indigenous population and the Africans brought as slaves to America. The proposal proved to be highly controversial. There were some who spoke of "suffering from a guilt complex", and would not support the idea.

Nevertheless, Pope John Paul II did so publicly, and a bishop took up the theme in a morning liturgy; a penitential service was organized by one of the base communities in Santo Domingo which some bishops attended. [10]

Liberation theologian Jan Sobrino commented later:

> In the sinful and hypocritical world of the North, which thinks it has no need to ask anybody for forgiveness, either for the violent deaths it caused in Vietnam, Afghanistan, El Salvador, Guatemala, Grenada, Panama, or the slow death it is inflicting on the south of the planet, asking for forgiveness is a good thing and purifies the air we breathe. [11]

But such an act has to be linked with a real commitment to effect the kind of change that will start undoing the long-term effects of colonialism. Indigenous peoples living in village or tribal groupings that were self-sustaining before colonization are now trapped in an economic system that keeps the majority of people poor.

Several liberation theologians and pastors have denounced capitalism. They are not alone. Other voices from the North join with them in this denunciation. The British publication *The New Internationalist* tells the tale of a tiny island in the Caribbean, the Emerald Isle of the Leewards, drawn "inexorably" into the international global economy and facing the nightmare scenario of becoming a dumping place for US toxic waste. [12] When the Bretton Woods conference met fifty years ago to begin to create a global economy, British economist John Maynard Keynes warned that the proposed system — biased highly in favour of global competition and corporate enterprise — would "inevitably lead to inequalities and instabilities". And he was right.

An Indian professor leads ten million farmers in a modern-day "peasants revolt" to protest against the signing of the latest round of the General Agreement on Tariffs and Trade. In particular the farmers were protesting against agreements which would mean they could no longer gather seeds from their crops, but would have to buy them from seed companies. This measure, Prof. Najundaswami told Walter Schwartz of *The Guardian*, would threaten the livelihood of all but rich farmers. "Our farms are our last refuge. If we are driven off we suffer extermination. What is happening in sub-Saharan Africa will happen here." [13]

"I believe that the world will improve when the little one who suffers starts to believe in the strength of the little ones." These words are from a hymn sung often in the BECs in Brazil, a hymn that is a favourite of Dom Helder Camara, the archbishop of Olinda and Recife in the northeast of Brazil, himself such an outspoken critic of capitalism. It is this action of empowerment that has been such a primary contribution of the grassroots communities, whether in Latin America, Africa, Asia or among the poor and marginalized of the North. A story from the base communities in Latin America that has been told repeatedly in the North is of a small group of women in Brazil who met together regularly to study the Bible. They were reading Luke's account of the birth of Jesus and were moved by this story of a poor family constantly on the move, whose baby had to be born in a stable. It led to a long discussion on the injustices, humiliations and hardships that they as mothers had experienced themselves. They knew of a neighbour whose baby was born while she was waiting in a queue to see the doctor, and the baby died. They knew of waiting in shops while better dressed people were served first, of being badly treated as domestic servants, of how difficult it was to feed their families because of high prices. One person asked, "Why did Jesus choose to be born poor and humble?" There was a long pause, and then another suggested: "Maybe... it was to show these rich people that *we* are important too." The story then tells how a "ripple of excitement went through the room. Was God really making such a clear statement about their humanity. About *their* rights as people?"

The buzz this caused in the room was stilled as another spoke up. "I think we still haven't got the complete answer to the question. I think God chose his Son to be born like us so that *we* can realize that we are important. It is not just to show the bosses. It is to show us too!" [14]

It is not only in the South that belief in one's self-worth is an issue. This was again one of the main concerns that came up time and again in the story-telling workshops I led in West Midlands and Leeds. These were workshops composed of two or more groups coming together to share their stories and interact with each other. The first workshop I held was for two groups: the Hope Community, "a kind of base community" situated on a housing estate in a multi-ethnic, deprived part of Wolverhampton, and Claiming the Inheritance, a grassroots movement among black Christians of different denominations whose aim is to raise the level of black consciousness.

They were two very different groups in many aspects. From the Hope Community came two sisters and a woman living on the estate, and all three happened to be white. From Claiming the Inheritance came a group of 14, women and men, young and older, all black. Their stories of discrimination and poverty, however, kept both groups attentive and eager to ask questions. At the end I asked them to flag up any similarities in their stories. "Helping people find self-esteem. Knowing their worth" was the Hope Community's answer. Claiming the Inheritance had a longer list, but there too figured "self-esteem and confidence".

In nearly all the workshops that followed, in both the West Midlands and Leeds, this matter of "knowing our worth" came up time and again. For me it is one of the most telling connections between the basic Christian communities, South and North. To be poor and marginalized, whatever form that may take, too easily robs one of any sense of personal value, and only those who know their worth have the courage and dignity to work for a better future — their own and that of others. Such knowledge comes when one knows one is valued by God and experiences that first-hand in a small, intimate group.

While working on this chapter, I received a mailing from Christian Aid. Included in it was a card to sign and send to the London office of the World Bank. I signed and sent it. It said that I understood that UK taxpayers give on average £10 to the World Bank and the International Monetary Fund each year, and asked how the World Bank spends its share of the money. In particular it asked how World Bank structural adjustment loans are used to tackle poverty in the third world. I am now waiting for their answer. I know my card was one of thousands. This is all part of Christian Aid's "Who Runs the World?" campaign to inform Christians in Britain and Ireland of the effects of structural adjustment conditions imposed on loans to third-world countries, and to draw them into their campaign for changed policies.

Posting a card is a little thing, but becoming more aware of issues is important. Little things also add up, particularly if there is a small basic group that is engaged in common action. The local justice and peace group to which I belong plans to focus on actions linked with a campaign against the arms trade. It will join with other campaigning groups and seek to draw in other Catholics and Anglicans in Poole and beyond.

For veteran campaigners there have been recent signs of hope — among them, the comparatively peaceful transition to a non-racial democracy in South Africa, and the World Development movement's successful challenge to the British government over their illegal use of aid money to pay a £234 million grant to the Pergau dam project in Malaysia. Both cases showed the increasing strength of "people power". In Britain more and more people are taking their grievances with the government to the streets and public places. Engaging in non-violent direct action are road protesters, pensioners, people with disabilities and animal rights activists. The intention of Dorset county council to install both a waste tip and an incinerator in or near the village where I live has energized the local community to just such non-violent protest. We will all be marching together!

Leonardo Boff has said that the heat has not yet been sufficiently turned on in Europe for any real liberation movement to emerge. That is still true, and yet perhaps not as true as it was. And in fact it may be the heat being turned down that will be the real trigger — a coldness. There is widespread disillusionment with the policies of the present government and scepticism that any other party can do better. More and more people are worried about the future, not only their own but that of the society in which we live. And our future and that of the South seem to be ever more inextricably bound up together. To see that alters one's perspective.

This matter of perspective was touched on in a very graphic way by Ed de la Torre, speaking at the 1991 Paris congress of European BCCs. He talked about birds and fishes, and what he said struck a deep chord with many of us there. The birds, Ed said, are like those who pay "flying visits" from the North to the South — journalists, development aid personnel, church leaders, even popes! They get an overview of many places and people, but it is easy for them to make sweeping judgments, to give "good" advice. The fishes on the other hand move slowly "through the water, which is thicker, colder, maybe even dirtier than the air". Birds cannot know what it is like to be fish by observation; they have to become like them — "feel the structures and culture that weigh down on people, including the memories of failure and frustration, disappointment and defeat". If they cannot be one of the fishes, they can learn from them. Then there can be a "coalition of birds and fishes" that can at least build a "countervailing power" that confronts and overcomes unjust power.

Spirituality for justice needs both renewal of energy and also new energies. We renew by meeting companions in the struggle, by reviving our sense of prophetic anger and also celebration... We find new energy in developing two-way solidarity between "birds" and "fishes", in both North and South.

"We may be coming from different places and situations," said one of the members of the discussion group I was in at Notre Dame. "That is not the issue. The issue is that we are all taking steps in the same direction. We are all at different stages on that path, but we are all open to be converted. Our goal is to change society, but this is a big goal. We have to be realistic about what we can or cannot contribute to that in our own basic Christian community. But together we can have an impact on society."

NOTES

[1] Letter from basic Christian communities present at the sixth inter-ecclesial gathering of BCCs, Trinidade, July 1986.

[2] Pope Paul VI, April 1969, quoted by Cesar Herrera in *Word Event*, nos 62-63, 1986. Publication of the World Catholic Federation for the Biblical Apostolate.

[3] *Word Event*, *ibid.*

[4] *Living the Good News, Lent 1992*, London, Christian Aid, CAFOD and SCIAF, 1991.

[5] *Word Event*, *op. cit.*

[6] "Journeys in Central America", Dave and Tina Cave, 1989.

[7] "Renewal from the Roots", report of a RCL/WCC team visit to Brazil, May-June 1988.

[8] Geneva, WCC, 1991, p.17.

[9] Ched Myers, *Who Will Roll Away the Stone*, Maryknoll, New York, Orbis, 1994.

[10] *Santo Domingo and After: The Challenge for the Latin American Church*, London, CIIR, 1993.

[11] *Ibid*.

[12] July 1994 issue.

[13] Walter Schwarz, "Seeds of Discontent", *The Guardian*, 11 March 1994.

[14] *Living the Good News*, *op. cit.*

6. Remaking History from Beneath

"The church of the future will be one built from below by basic communities as a result of free initiative and association," wrote the German theologian Karl Rahner in *The Shape of the Church to Come*. Rahner further stated that in his view if basic communities did not develop in this way then the "institutional church will shrivel up into a church without people".

Vincent Donovan writes in *The Church in the Midst of Creation* that everywhere he has heard the same question in one form or another: "We see quite plainly the church as it is, but what should it be like?" His own answer is given in the epilogue. Here a "forlorn group of black parishioners and a white priest" meet in a church office. They have come together to discuss the gospel according to Luke. Discussion proceeds awkwardly until a woman says how surprised she is that in the gospel story women spoke out so freely against the traditional way of doing things. This loosened tongues. Another meeting followed, and another. Numbers grew and more questions were asked and discussed. Questions were asked about the neighbourhoods in which the members lived. Ideas began to flow, and hope grew that change could happen in some of the dismal housing projects. In this way a basic Christian community was born.

Donovan writes that to join this community was to join a people struggling for freedom from oppression, persecution, meaninglessness; that they had started out with "a very naive and antiquated vision of the church and Christianity", but a change had taken place. They had taken on "a new appreciation of themselves. If Christ is black, then black is indeed beautiful. The blacks in the community began seeing themselves as important in the church, as necessary for the church, as the only hope of renewal for the church, as the heart of the revolution in organized Christianity for a refounding of the church of Christ in our age."

"The epilogue of this book, of course, never happened," Donovan tells us — adding "in one place".

Four years before the publication of this book in 1989, Bishop Julio X. Labayen of the Philippines, in the address cited in Chapter 2, had looked ahead and made his prediction:

> I guess or predict that the basic Christian communities or *comunidades de base* will prove to be the major powerful influence in the church of the future. I predict they will affect the whole church as deeply as the growth of the monastic orders, the Benedictines for example, from the 5th century to the middle ages; or the Jesuits and the other apostolic orders from the 16th to the present century; or the evolution of the Protestant churches over the recent centuries.
>
> I foresee the church will form a consensus to promote the growth of the basic Christian communities, and this decision will be as important for the life of the church as the decision made by the council of Jerusalem to open the church to the Gentiles on the Gentiles' terms.

Is it likely that these theologians and pastors are predicting the future of the church correctly, that their prophetic insight is truly pointing the way ahead for us and coming generations? Julio de Santa Ana, writing in 1979, was cautious; it was too soon to make any prediction, he said, since the growth of the BCCs was too recent a development. There are, however, some important factors to consider.

Deeply rooted
The concept of basic Christian communities did not emerge as a new idea arising out of Vatican II; it predated it and indeed was one of the factors that helped give birth to the Council. While the pioneering BCCs which grew rapidly in Brazil following Vatican II are well-known, we saw in Chapter 1 that the seeds of such a movement can

already be identified in the mission of the "worker-priests" who emerged in France in the 1940s and elsewhere in Europe after the second world war. It was a vision that had taken a long time to come to fruition. As early as 1929, Cardinal Suhard had said: "There is a whole region around Caen, containing all our great factories, where Christ is unknown; this is our true mission territory. Day and night this haunts me; I long for missionaries."[1] In 1941 he founded the Mission de France, a seminary to prepare priests to work effectively in working-class areas.

Worker-priests did not gain official recognition until 1964 when Pope Paul VI gave his qualified approval. It is the worker-priest movement that is identified by present members as the origin of BCCs in France. Both symbolically and concretely, the continued use of the "pastoral cycle" (see — judge — act) by base communities worldwide attests to the close connection between the two movements.

There are other similar roots. The Iona community with its centre on the isle of Iona in Scotland was founded in the 1930s by George MacLeod, at that time a young Presbyterian minister working in the slums of Glasgow. MacLeod had been challenged by both the severe hardships of many people living in Glasgow in the depression of the 1930s and their alienation from the church. He decided to rebuild the ancient abbey of Iona, using the practical skills of workmen from his area of Govan in Glasgow. It was a way of bringing together faith and practical work, of gaining strength to tackle afresh the problems of daily life in Glasgow. It led in time to the forming of the Iona community, a dispersed community of people living in Scotland and England, meeting regularly in small family groups for prayer, reflection and action, with the rebuilt abbey on the isle of Iona as a centre for community and guests to come to throughout the year.

Ian Fraser, who was himself a worker-priest ("before the first worker-priests even began") sees the Iona community as a pioneer of basic Christian communities. "It stands as a John-the-Baptist sign of what was to follow. In the 1930s it was charting a road ahead on which many others would later travel."[2] But it is not only a sign; its present-day family groups are themselves basic Christian communities.

The Corrymeela community in Northern Ireland is closely associated with the Iona community, and is structured in the same way with a residential centre and family groups dispersed throughout Northern Ireland. In these communities and others scattered throughout Ireland, Scotland, Wales and parts of England, the roots are deeply Celtic, and their emphasis on what is small, communal, participatory and concerned with the everyday tasks and issues of life is true to the Celtic church tradition.

Methodism is another root, with its small cells that originally made up the Methodist church. Now in Britain there is a new programme, Grassroots, working to renew and revitalize this concept of "church" within British Methodism, drawing on the assistance of overseas Partners in Mission.

Both in concept and in the actual outworking, the forerunners are endless. The writings of Karl Barth, Rudolf Bultmann, Paul Tillich and Dietrich Bonhoeffer are among the many sources from which liberation theologians have drawn insights. The remaking of history from beneath — "a repressed but resurgent theology" — is recognized by Gutiérrez as a long journey with many milestones. He sees awareness of this continuity as an essential task:

> The great milestones of this long journey have to be studied — the primitive Christian community, the great pastors and theologians of the first centuries, the Franciscan movement and Joachim de Fiore in the middle ages, the Hussite

movement in the 15th century, the peasant wars in Germany and Thomas Münzer in the 16th, the defence of the Indians by Bartolomé de las Casas, Bishop Juan del Valle, and so many others of the same era in Latin America, Juan Santos Atahualpa in the 18th century in Peru, and the peasant struggles and popular piety in more recent times in Latin America.[3]

Ultimately it is the primitive Christian community that inspires and encourages the basic Christian communities. An integral part of the Marins workshops is the early church exercise. By the time this exercise is reached, participants have already formed small groups or communities. Each group is given the name of a church — Antioch, Jerusalem, Corinth. Having previously read given texts, they piece together the story of that church, taking on the roles of the different characters. Then they begin to spread out, one going to Antioch, another to Rome and so on, in each place to share their story. Always one or more members of the group stay at home to welcome visitors. Out of the sharing of similarities and differences, a lively debate ensues. Each group shares bread and wine; how they do this is their decision. Towards the end of the time, the participants again come together to debrief. Always there is a profound wonder at the new insights that have been gained, at how close to their own concerns is the early church story, at the richness gained from — in modern terms — networking. And a renewed commitment to work at this "new way of being church".

Authentic discipleship

Driving through the gates into Maryknoll to take part in the orientation programme in November 1991, I looked, and looked again. It was so vast, a village all to itself with, as I was to discover later, its own post office. Inside the building, everything was just as grand, and entering the dining room for our first meal we were presented with enormous choice. Vast, grandiose, big, rich — not what I expected at a consultation on small Christian communities. Part of my reaction I knew was the stereotyped British response — "everything is so big in the USA" — but it was more than that: I was struggling with what I believed about Christian discipleship, about simplicity, evangelical poverty, solidarity with the poor and the marginalized.

The second day I took a walk. It was then that I came to Memorial Corner and, reading the names, came across those of Maura Clarke and Ita Ford, Maryknoll sisters who had been abducted and murdered in 1980 by the Salvadorean national guard. I returned to the building in a different frame of mind. I had been reminded that all over the world there are Maryknollers who are serving the worldwide church, many of them in base communities and in places where people still face persecution, torture and death. I was sobered by that reminder, and it enabled me to hear what the seminary staff said: "When our missionaries come home we want them to eat well, and to rest."

That picture of the memorial stayed in my mind as I travelled to Notre Dame for the actual consultation. It was soon to become larger and more poignant. The Latin Americans had brought with them photographs — faces of women and men, most often young people, who had died at the hands of paid assassins or the equivalent of the Salvadorean national guard in other countries. At one eucharist we were each given a photograph to hold while the celebration was taking place. Before the consecration other photographs were placed on the floor to form a large cross. Theirs were not names any of us knew; they were not public figures. They were sons and daughters, mothers and fathers, friends and companions, members of basic Christian communities, some priests, some religious, but mostly lay women and men.

In El Salvador over 7000 cases were investigated by the commission set up following the peace accords on the basis of direct testimony, as well as a further 18,000 whose names came from secondary sources. They included Archbishop Oscar Romero, four US church-women (Ita Ford, Maura Clarke, Dorothy Kazel and Jean Donovan) and six Jesuits massacred together with their cook and her daughter. One of these Jesuits, Ignacio Ellacuria, had been rector of the Central American University of El Salvador and one of Archbishop Romero's theological advisers. The same situation existed in Brazil, Guatemala, Chile, Colombia and the Philippines, and continues today in Haiti, East Timor and quite a few other places.

Why kill all these Christians? "The persecution of the church — the murder, torture and harassment of clergy and laity — is a reaction to its support of the poor and landless rural population." CAMINO (Central America Information Office) is certain of this fact, and its "Background to the Crisis" provides detailed information.

"I will try to learn some Spanish in preparation for our next gathering," I told a Peruvian woman in my discussion group at Notre Dame. We had become friends. I felt close to her, but wanted to be able to communicate with her more directly. "No, better you say what you want now," she replied. "In two years I may be dead." She was not being dramatic; it was said in a matter-of-fact way, as a given.

Earthed spirituality

The story-telling workshops I ran in the West Midlands and in Leeds were a way of collecting stories of basic Christian communities emerging in the British context. The groups were very different: small groups finding new ways to be church on inner-city housing estates, an Anglican church choosing "to change course and provide an open door to the community around it", rural churches seeking new ways of shared ministry, a "doing theology" group, a group of black Christians seeking to raise black consciousness among their own people, an ecumenical group responding to social need, a group building community with homeless women and men and another forming caring relationships with prostitutes. In the West Midlands a common factor in all the groups had been their attendance some time previously at a Marins workshop. In Leeds a local group working in the areas of caring, justice and social concern helped me make contact with the groups.

At the workshops the groups told their stories, questioned each other, and at the end worked on similarities and areas of common concern.

> Small, ordinary, but get there
> Making the way by walking
> Starting from real need
> Taking risks
> Being on the margins
> Being misunderstood
> Journeying — no fixed goals
> People-centred
> Enabling people to attain their own dignity to realize their own worth and value and to grow as individuals

This is just a sample from the many lists made of similarities. Although these groups and communities are very different from one another in so many ways, they have so much in common. This commonality was commented on at all the workshops. At one workshop when the similarities were written up on the flip chart, there was an awed silence. One person broke into tears.

In discovering what is held in common, different groups felt authenticated in their own journey. It was encouraging to sense that in and beyond their own small venture something was definitely stirring in the church — church taken here in the broadest sense.

In 1988 when I compiled a report on renewal movements in Britain I wrote:

> What is found here is a search for and hunger for a truly authentic kind of Christian life-style, a more radical commitment to the values that Jesus taught. From what I have read and heard people say... it is only such an authentic Christian life-style that is going to be able to command the attention and respect of those outside. It is the essence of mission. Those on the fringes are the pioneers. The challenge to the mainstream is not how can it bring these back into the fold, but how can it best learn from them.[4]

It was this same search that drew me in the 1960s to seek baptism in the Spirit and to become part of the charismatic renewal, which led me to help found a Christian community in the village where I live. It was this same hunger that was touched when I read of the grass-roots communities: a hunger for reality, for an earthed spirituality. And it was this hunger that I saw in people's eyes when in 1986 I travelled with Jim Wallis, editor of *Sojourners* magazine, to meetings held in England, Scotland and Wales. So many of those who heard Jim's message of a radical Christian life-style wanted to know how to find the people, the places, the situations where this kind of spirituality could be lived. Not as one individual or even as one family, but with others in community.

In the wake of countless mergers and take-overs in the British publishing world, which had adversely affected Christian publishing as well as secular, the Student Christian Movement published in 1990 a provocative article entitled "Where Will We Find Light for the Dark Ages?" The changes in Christian publishing about which they wrote — that in future it would be the market and not a social commitment that would dictate what books would be published — was only the background to what they wished most to say:

> There are other Christians. We do not hear so much of them because they have little voice, and when we hear from them they begin by saying that they feel isolated and alone. No longer regular members of the main churches, though by no means uninterested in religion, Christian concerns and beliefs, and often with a deep sense of God and a commitment to making ours a better world, they are the result of a distinctive phenomenon of our time.

The newsletter in which the article was published had asked for some response, and mentioned the possibility of a kind of informal network. The response was a deluge — over a thousand letters. The newsletter had touched a nerve end — the search of many outside the institutional church to meet with others to explore issues of concern theologically. One result has been a network of small groups across the country meeting informally in homes to do just this.

Gwen Cashmore and Joan Puls are co-directors of the Ecumenical Spirituality Project of the Council of Churches for Britain and Ireland. They have travelled many times throughout England, Ireland, Scotland and Wales, meeting small ecumenical communities, councils of churches, local ecumenical projects and informal home groups. They have had a unique opportunity to find out what Christians in Britain are thinking and wanting. They have concluded:

> There are numerous signs today of a yearning for something broad enough and deep enough to contain and to channel the hopes and struggles, the questions, aspirations and heartaches of ordinary people. There is a thirst for new and more relevant styles of liturgy and of prayer, for more interface between faith in word and faith in deed, for a sense of

solidarity in confronting both global and local concerns, for ways of belonging to one another across boundaries of denomination, culture and background. There is serious questioning because of the stagnancy and irrelevancy of many of our religious rituals and church traditions.

Many people feel undernourished, neglected, even rejected. They long for something which releases them into their heritage, the freedom of the children of God, something which widens their horizons and challenges their half-hearted convictions.

New forms of partnership

"I wouldn't be a Catholic any more if it had not been for the small Christian community," a member of one of the Upper Saddle River SCCs told us. And for many, denominational allegiance or indeed membership of any church has become irrelevant; their search is for something else, something more basic. It is not for any form of church as such, but for a way to live, to be — as church.

There are others — religious, clerics and lay Christians of different denominations — who are members of such groups and have not abandoned denominational membership, but they hold more loosely to it. They are discovering how closely they are bound to sisters and brothers of other denominations, how much is held in common.

This kind of ecumenism is easier to achieve than at the institutional level. Julio de Santa Ana writes about this in *Towards a Church of the Poor*: "It is an ecumenism of the people, an ecumenism of the poor which does not care about the formal aspects of Christian unity or inter-religious/inter-ideological dialogues, an ecumenism of people who believe that institutional ecumenism should follow what is being practised instead of claiming to set the norms..."[5] Indeed, it is an ecumenism that goes further and embraces those of other faiths and none, recognizing in all people of good will the face of God.

There could be the sense here that institutional ecumenism has now been left so far behind that its efforts can
only become increasingly meaningless. This, however, is
not thought to be the case by all — indeed by many — at
the grassroots. The challenge is presented to the institution
to be constantly reviewing and clarifying what it is about
in the light of what is happening at the base, but the
challenge would be all one way.

What is seen as important is the need to find new
forms of partnership between movement and institution.
The institution offers stability, tradition, scholarship,
expertise — and resources: buildings, personnel, money.
When the vitality and experience of the base groups come
together with the resources of the institution a powerful
force for good is set in motion. This was evident in the
beginnings of the base communities in Latin America. It is
sustaining this kind of relationship that is often difficult,
and yet it is certain to become ever more essential as time
goes on.

Those taking part in the 1995 European seminar of
basic Christian communities will meet in plenary in the
hall of the Ecumenical Centre in Geneva. A small thing,
but symbolically important — perhaps signifying some
new possibilities for the future. In the beginning of the
Christian base movement in the 1960s the Catholic church
in Latin America helped the communities to grow by
helping with publications, teaching manuals, and training
of lay leaders. That was in predominantly Catholic countries. The Better World Movement which helped to bring
about the growth of BCCs in these countries found that
similar approaches did not work in others where there was
a greater denominational mix, and where there was usually also greater secularization. For one thing it was
essential that different churches in an area found a way to
work together if there was to be an effective revitalization
of local communities. In such countries where no one

denomination is in the majority, only the ecumenical agencies can take on such a supportive role — promoting and helping in the formation of basic Christian communities. Such a creative partnership, however, has exciting possibilities.

A new way of being church

An English Catholic bishop, Cormac Murphy O'Connor, wrote in 1983 that twenty years previously he had been greatly influenced by a book written by the theologian Yves Congar, *Lay People in the Church*. Bishop Murphy O'Connor, writing about the meaning of small Christian communities, quoted from it:

> They (small Christian communities) answer a need to rediscover the church and, in a sense, to re-enter and renew her from below. Many of our contemporaries find that for them the church's machinery, sometimes the very institution, is a barrier obscuring her deep and living mystery, which they can find, or find again, only from below, through little church cells wherein the mystery is lived directly and with great simplicity. A need is felt to seek, beneath the ready-made administrative machinery, the living reality of basic communities..., a community to whose life all its members contribute and which is patterned by give-and-take and a pooling of resources. [6]

In his diocese, the Roman Catholic diocese of Arundel and Brighton, a formation programme of basic Christian communities has existed since 1971. A new way of being church.

The 19th-century French poet, mystic and visionary Charles Péguy foresaw such a transformation. It was a part of his dream. "The chief thing that needs remaking, the most important of all, is the parish."

He talked about "praying the parish" into being and searched throughout his life to know more clearly his parish-to-be. Alan Ecclestone in his study of Péguy, *A*

Staircase to Silence, draws a picture of the kind of parish he dreamed of.

> A parish means a body of people drawn and held together in a spirit that prompts the members to care for, respect and love each other... Small enough to permit a true understanding to grow up between its members. Such a body... would ever be seeking to do two kinds of work; the one within itself in relating its members ever more genuinely to each other in love, the other in shaping a common attitude towards the life of the world in which it is situated. Learning to speak the truth together in love, its members would form a community not withdrawn from but actively engaged with the world, and experiencing in an ever deepening fashion a communion of transcendent character.

Charles Péguy died soon after the turn of the century, some sixty or so years before the growth of basic Christian communities would become apparent, but in the coming into being of these communities Alan Ecclestone sees the new kind of parish that Péguy prayed for.

Moving in the same direction

"We are living in a vacuum."

That statement has become a truism; one's eyes flicker across the page and move on to the next sentence. The words are here again, however, in bold lettering across the page in the 14 January 1995 edition of *The Guardian*, announcing a new feature to run several weeks, a debate on what might fill the vacuum in British politics. The following week Will Hutton, *The Guardian*'s economic editor, responded to the first article. His opening sentences declared: "Britain's national affairs are reaching explosive levels of stress. The individualist laissez-faire values which imbue the economic and political elite have been found wanting — but with the decline of socialism, there seems to be no coherent alternative."

This is the case not only in Britain; it is so throughout the Western world. In the late 1980s we sat glued to our television screens and watched, amazed, as the communist system of state socialism fell apart bit by bit. It seemed so strong, so frighteningly invulnerable. Now we watch in disbelief as day after day we are told that we too are in trouble. A recent WCC publication tells of a senior European foreign affairs official who admitted to a church delegation in Brussels that "he did not know what was to be done, adding significantly that 'there is no guarantee that the market system will survive'". [7]

If the future of the social and economic fabric of our lives is shifting and changing, is it likely that the church can stay the same and survive? But survival is not really what is at stake; what is at stake is a church that can help shape what is to come. Jim Wallis, speaking at the Sojourners Britain and Ireland first national gathering in 1994, challenged us to see "the church as the midwife" of a new society. It can be that, but will it be?

Some years back I was walking along the shoreline of Poole Harbour close to where I live. What did I believe of the future, where did I want to put my energies? These were questions I was asking myself at the time. And another question came to my mind: How does change happen? I pondered over this, and concluded that change comes primarily from those who want it most, who know through bitter experience that life can and should be different. I thought of a great-aunt whom I never met. She had been a suffragette, she was one of that band of women who were desperate enough to chain themselves to the railings and face all that was slung at them — in order to bring about change. Change, I saw, came from below, from a thrusting upwards of those desiring to be born and to give birth to a new situation, a new society. I concluded then that that was where I wanted to be: to position myself at the grassroots, with the dispossessed, the marginalized.

I was naive enough at that time to think that I alone had stumbled on some amazing new insight! How much better it was to discover, as time went on, that I was part of a shift in consciousness happening worldwide.

It is here — at the grassroots — that the basic Christian communities are to be found. They are not alone, they are part of a vast number of groups, communities, initiatives, projects, organizations — secular, Christian, Buddhist, Hindu, Muslim — all moving in the same direction. All part of what Jim Douglass calls "a peaceful revolution". [8]

Who would not want to be part of this movement?

NOTES

[1] Peter Hebblethwaite, *John XXIII, Pope of the Council*, London, Cassell, 1984.

[2] Ian Fraser, *Living a Countersign*, Glasgow, Wild Goose Publications, 1990.

[3] Gustavo Gutiérrez, *The Power of the Poor in History*, London, SCM, 1983.

[4] Jeanne Hinton, *Overview of Present Day Renewal Movements within the Church in Britain*, compiled for Mennonite Board of Missions, USA, 1988.

[5] Geneva, WCC, 1979.

[6] Cormac Murphy O'Connor, *The Family of the Church*, London, Darton, Longman & Todd, 1984.

[7] Alastair Hulbert, "Hints and Guesses", in *Hear What the Spirit Says to the Churches*, ed. Gerhard Linn, Geneva, WCC, 1994, p.9.

[8] James W. Douglass, *The Nonviolent Coming of God*, Maryknoll, NY, Orbis, 1991.

Afterword: The New Kairos

"It is by walking that we make a path," says an ancient Spanish proverb. But the pace of walking, it would appear, has slowed down. "For us in Brazil it is a tired moment," a young Brazilian told us at Notre Dame in 1991. "Energy is flagging; it is enough to put bread on the table."

A number of changes had happened by the 1990s. In many Latin American countries repressive military regimes had been replaced by democratically elected governments. This presented the communities with new challenges. At the same time the opposition of many in the Catholic hierarchy to the communities was beginning to take its toll. This opposition had been apparent even before Medellín in 1968, and at Puebla in 1979 liberation theologians were not even invited to take part in the deliberations. They made their contribution, however, staying in small guest houses nearby and burning the midnight oil writing out their responses to conference papers. But quite a few bishops were in sympathy with them and used their insights, and the influence of liberation theologians was evident in the final documents.

This was not enough, however, to halt the gathering opposition to liberation theologians or to the communities with which they had a close relationship. The measures taken by the Vatican to curtail their influence included the replacing of progressive bishops by conservative ones, especially in places where the communities were numerous and active, and the censoring of liberation theologians. (From the start these communities had been able to rely on the support and active help of bishops, priests and religious. While nuns and priests would take a back seat in the actual leadership of the community, they were nevertheless available as a resource and as an accreditation of the community to the wider church. The links with the institutional church had never been broken.) Gradually other resources were also withdrawn. There were deliberate staff changes at CELAM (Latin American Episcopal Conference) that resulted in the loss of valuable financial and other support. Measures like these were to add up and contribute to the "tired moment".

The fourth general conference of Latin American bishops, at Santo Domingo in 1993, was watched closely by many, not least to see how the communities would fare. The conclusions of the conference emphasize a "new way of evangelizing", and reaffirm the preferential option for the poor. Other statements, however, give some idea of the tensions that have emerged. The communities are "a living cell of the parish", and attempts are to be made "to integrate them into the parish". Observers commented afterwards that there seemed to be a concerted attempt to turn the communities into "just another parish group", no different from any other. They are no longer "a new way of being church".[1]

In 1994 Peter Price, general secretary of the United Society for the Propagation of the Gospel (USPG), re-visited a base community in a *favela* in Sao Paulo. When he first visited the community in 1987 he found it "vibrant with activity". The community had been engaged in providing sewerage for the slum, building a children's creche and working together to bring about political and social change. Now in 1994 he found a different commu-nity — smaller, disheartened, on the defensive.

He found also that in Brazil the base communities were losing ground to the Pentecostals. But by a strange turn of events the Pentecostals had developed an agenda similar to the communities: they were engaging in rural unions and the struggle for land rights. "An emerging vision might be some rapprochement leading to a move-ment that is profoundly Christian, politically radical and socially communitarian," concludes Price.[2]

This possibility is also seen by Victor Codina, who also points to the growing similarities between Pentecos-

104

tals and the base communities. "It opens up possibilities for a new grassroots ecumenism," he writes. He senses internal changes within the communities as a result of all these pressures, but he sees them as hopeful.

> The base communities, with the wisdom characteristic of the people, and specifically of women, have realized that what is important now is not to repeat models or slogans of the past that do not meet the needs of the present, but to live the new kairos in today's new socio-economic and church context... Some people will certainly see this new style as an abandonment of the primitive ideal of the base communities. In fact it is a step forward, not a step back...
>
> Latin America's base communities, even though not all of them are conscious of this or can put it into words, are assisting at the birth of an alternative model of society and church, creating alternative visions to the neo-liberalism of today and to the revolutionary ideas of the 1970s, visions that can energize society and church. [3]

A shared utopia

A Catholic priest who had helped to bring a crisis in one community to a fruitful resolution was asked if he minded that his part in it was barely recognized. "No," he said, "it is always so when one has chosen to work at the base." The story of the Christian base communities is often the same; they are indeed like leaven or salt. But here and there in news columns, magazines and television documentaries, the stories filter through; in particular in 1994 those of Mexico, East Timor and Haiti. East Timorese resistance groups campaigned to have the Catholic Church in East Timor nominated for the 1994 Nobel peace prize, for the role of priests, nuns and lay workers in defending the rights of the people since Indonesia's invasion of East Timor in 1975. Another nominee for the Nobel peace prize is Mexico's Bishop Samuel Ruiz of San Cristobal de las Casas, who has long defended the rights of the peasants and indigenous people of Chiapas. A graphic picture is drawn of thousands of impoverished Indians who can neither read nor write leaving their fields untended and walking for days in order to affix their thumbprints on petitions in support of Bishop Ruiz. Walking with them are lay workers and members of base communities.[4] In Haiti a Montfordian priest, Fr Jean-Marie Vincent, a friend of Jean-Bertrand Aristide, is gunned down outside his home in Port au Prince. He too was considered too radical, too dangerous. Too dangerous perhaps because he also was not acting on his own, but represented countless others who walk this way of being church.

In less volatile circumstances others look at the road ahead. In April 1994 the African Catholic bishops had their own synod in Rome. What was most significant about it, commentators agreed, was the consensus reached. It came up with its own image or model of church — "the church as family, which in practice implies the creation of small communities at the human level, living or basic ecclesial communities".[5] Earlier in the synod the bishops had spoken of such SCCs as ideal cells for promoting justice and peace — "an expression of African communitarianism". Indeed, one bishop from Mozambique had declared that in his view "any pastoral strategy that omitted small Christian communities would be creating a church without a future".

We move on. We are not sure of the destination — who can be? From the pastoral department for small Christian communities in the archdiocese of Hartford, USA, comes a spring 1995 reflection book for small Christian communities. The commentary at one point reads:

> Lent urges us to move to the margins, to dwell at the fringe — where we do not have it all together — to wait for the in-breaking of God. Lent invites us to loosen our grip, to let go

of so much we think we have to hold on to so tightly, to open our arms to receive.

It is dark at the edges. We fear we are alone. But it is the witness of the gospel that God spoke to the disciples when they were overshadowed by a cloud and were afraid.

I am encouraged too by the words of Helder Camara:

We should not be afraid of utopia. I like to repeat that, when we dream alone, we limit ourselves merely to dreams. When we dream together with others, we immediately reach the realm of reality. The utopia which we share with others is like the bed of the river of human history. [6]

NOTES

[1] Victor Codina, "The Wisdom of Latin America's Base Communities", in *Mysticism and the Institutional Crisis*, eds. C. Duquoc and G. Gutiérrez (*Concilium*, 4), London, SCM, 1994.

[2] Peter Price, *Transmission*, USPG quarterly publication, 1 November 1994.

[3] Codina, *loc. cit.*

[4] Bill and Patty Coleman, "Bishop in the Middle", *The Tablet*, 12 October 1994.

[5] Report in *The Tablet*, 23 April 1994.

[6] Quoted by Julio de Santa Ana, "Is There Hope for the Third World", Amsterdam, Vrije Universiteit, 1988.